The Art of
Split-Second Success

THE ART OF
SPLIT-SECOND SUCCESS

HOW TO ACT FAST AND CREATE POSITIVE RESULTS NOW!

Robert Channing

ISBN-13: 9780692682715
ISBN-10: 0692682716
Library of Congress Control Number: 2016938249
Power Performers Publishing, Washington Mills, NY

WHAT PEOPLE ARE SAYING
ABOUT ROBERT CHANNING...

"Robert Channing has helped raise more than $150 million for charity alongside President Bill Clinton, Christina Aguilera, and Mariah Carey with YUM Brands! and the United Nations "From Hunger to Hope." Robert is THE most amazing man I have ever met and had the privilege to work with in my life!"

—David Novak, CEO, YUM! Brands, Taco Bell, KFC, Pizza Hut

"No! Stop! That's bananas... I Love It! Robert – Thank you so much! I'm going to put your painting up in my home! Amazing!!"

—Serena Williams, World's Women Tennis Champ

"12 years ago I hired Robert, I was so amazed that I've been telling everyone about him for 12 years. I'm now the CEO of a new company and we brought him in and he was absolutely amazing. Robert, Thank you, you stole the show!"

—Michael Cornell, CEO HighJump

"You couldn't have picked a better subject than me to paint. Love your work, what detail! Amazing! Thank you... your painting is going in a special place in my home!!"
"Robert you are unbelievable! What an amazing presentation it was like nothing I've ever seen before."

—Howard Stern, "King of All Media" Howard Stern Show

"Robert what an amazing presentation, I want you on our team! Just the best!"

—Spencer Rascoff, CEO Zillow

"That's me folks, I'm the Golden Child! That's HOT Robert! What an artist! Thank you for closing my TV special with a WOW at Universal Studios Orlando. You are truly an AMAZING guy!!"

—Steve Harvey, Comedian, Host - The Steve Harvey Show

"Amazing! Mind-boggling! Inspirational! Three standing ovations! What more can you ask for? Robert Channing's show is out of this world! A great alternative for a keynote speaker."

—Richard Boyle, VP Marketing, Johnson & Johnson

"A total success! Expect something phenomenal with your meeting or event using Robert Channing. It was spontaneous combustion on stage and in the audience during our corporate seminar. Mr. Channing came

highly recommended and what a show. Just ask us here at Kraft Foods and we will be more than happy to let you know. Unbelievable!"

—Charlene Brown, General Sales Manager—HR, Kraft Foods

"Your performance packed in more motivation and entertainment than we ever imagined...we look forward to working with Robert in the near future!"

—Deb Camren-Anderson, Event Show Manager, Motorola

"Investment bankers are generally a skeptical audience, but you managed to entertain, command their interest and keep them talking about your performance for days afterward. Your bent spoons have been a collector's item in our firm."

—Debra Douglas, Managing Director, CIBC World Markets

"WOW! What an amazing performance! Now how can you help me with my career?"

—Jimmy Fallon, *The Tonight Show Starring Jimmy Fallon*

"Thank you for helping us raise more than $250,000 for the CURE with your mental art performance and speed painting show. Truly a gift! Thank you, thank you, thank you."

—Suzanne Axelrod, Founding Chair, CURE for Epilepsy

"Thank you so much for speaking to LandAmerica OneStop at our recent planning meeting. Your entire program was unbelievable! I must say, while I had anticipated that your presentation would be interesting, I never expected to be so overwhelmed. Not only were you entertaining, you turned a room full of skeptics into a room full of believers that anything is possible. You certainly gave us a reason to believe the power of the mind is a tool to be used to our advantage. Thank you so much for making our event memorable."

—Cheryl Cox, President, LandAmerica OneStop

"Robert's show was the most amazing show I have seen in my LIFE!"

—Margo Lion, Producer of the hit Broadway show *Hairspray*

"Just amazing...Elmira College events are memorable because of Robert Channing, 165 shows and counting. See you next year. Thank you so much!"

—David Williams, Dean of Student Life, Elmira College NY

"Robert Channing is a refreshing alternative to conventional entertainment...He awes his audience and leaves them wanting more. His flexibility and personal touch makes his performance a memorable experience and fit for all types of conference formals."

—Michele Bloom, Meeting Planner, ECRM Select

"I loved it! I want you to paint me next time! AMAZING!"

—Heidi Klum, Supermodel and fashion icon

"Robert's performance was spectacular. Our audience was engaged, entertained and amazed from beginning to end, and they couldn't stop talking about his performance and talk after the show. Thanks for making our event such a success."

—Sandy Medved, Account Director, Wynford CN

Dedication

To my beautiful wife, Brenda: Thank you for being so supportive of me and my many endeavors over the years. You are the wind beneath my wings. I appreciate you sticking with me through the good times and bad. I love you dearly.

To my smart, beautiful, and loving children, Gabrielle Rose, Alexander Robert, Garrett Michael, and my little baby Mitchell Avery—who is playing in heaven with his grandparents and all the children whom God has taken too early from us: You are the reasons why I work so hard. I have always said to you that "Books unlock the secrets to the universe." This book is written for you. I hope that long after my time, you and your children will benefit from this destiny message. I love you all.

To my parents, Bob and Donna Johnson: You are the best parents a child could ask for. I have become the person I am today because of you. Thank you for all the positive words of encouragement that you have so kindly spoken to me throughout my entire life—I was always listening. I have benefited not only from all that you have given me, but also from all that you could not. I love you both. (Dad is in heaven with my son Mitchell.)

To you, the reader: It is my honor and privilege to help you discover and create your own destiny. Remember: Anything that your mind can conceive and you truly believe in your heart, you can achieve. Make it so, and really enjoy your lives to the fullest.

A special acknowledgment to my Power Performers staff: Debbie Kinsella who's my right arm, and the best sister I could ever have; Steve

Guy, "King of Loyal and Superstar Salesman;" Lisa Martin, "Queen of Power Performers and Sales Superstar;" and M.J. Amelio, my mother-in-law and past president of Power Performers, we miss you every day. Thank you all for making my career and yours a success. You serve our clients and friends *every* day in the world of meetings and events. To your success!

Acknowledgements

ANY SUCCESSFUL ENTREPRENEUR knows that there are more people than you can count who have contributed to and inspired any sort of lasting success. Here is my list, though I am sure I have left some people off from the last 27 years, but not intentionally. Many thanks to Rev. Russell Little, Les Leviness, Grandma Helen Johnson, Bill and Debbie Kinsella, Attorney George F. Aney, Garry L. Outtrim, Frank Madia, Rich Reynolds, Sandi Barry, Nancye Scymour, Adam Christing, Barb Christing, Mark Levy, Peter Economy, Michelle Weakley, Lisa Gensheimer, Michael Levine, Michael Plescia Jr., Michael and Cheryl Plescia, Bill and Debbie Kinsella, Jim Raymer, Chuck Obenesser, Jay Abraham, Scott Hallman, Dave Boufford, Joe Vitale, Chet Holmes, Russ Muthig, Jim Johnson, Sharon Keep, Paul Kroll, Kelly Yacco, Glen Fonner, Chris Martin, Foster Fahey, Rocco Fernald, Denny Dent, David Copperfield, Greg Frewin, Mike Moody, Joanne Reynolds Bladek, Walter Cummings, Blake and Cathy Ford, Bill Dustin, Jeff Sterling, Tony Labrosee, William Ortlieb, Tom Moran, Helen and Gary Plescia, Andy Howlett, Karen Carey, Bill Keeler, Gary Spears, Tad Pole and Polly Wog, Symeon and Shelly Tsoupelis, The Carbone Auto Group, Joe Carbone, Alex Carbone, Enessa Carbone, Rob Perry, Jim Lafountain, Jim Ellis, John Calabrese, Mike and Kelly Parsons, Nick Laino Jr., Shanon McEvoy, Jamie Carney, Mike Tasovac, Sam Licari, Michael Ciancaglini, Rob Czrew, Marty Greenfield, David Cuccinata, Mr. and Mrs. Frank Basil, Richard Venezio, Dr. Mark and Elise Finer, Dr. De Jesus, John McEntee, and all my friends at over the 3,000 colleges and universities and 900 corporations and associations I've spoken and performed for throughout my almost 30 years in business. Thank You All!

Table of Contents

INTRODUCTION

I MAKE MY living as a speed painter and mind artist, so I know something about making decisions and taking action fast.

I'll be on stage at a business conference in front of thousands of people, and an audience member will yell out what picture she wants me to paint. They'll shout things like, "The Statue of Liberty!" Or they'll scream the name of the U.S. president, or the name of their company's CEO.

A few seconds earlier, I had no idea what I was going to be asked to paint. Now I do. I grab my brushes, turn to a large onstage easel, and hurriedly cover the canvas in lines and paint. Four minutes later, I toss aside the brushes. I'm done.

From my canvas, the person or object called for is staring back at the audience in vivid color.

To go from a blank canvas to an artful painting in the time it takes most people to wolf down a slice of pizza on the run is not something anyone in the audience has ever seen before. More often than not, they rise to their feet—loudly applauding.

When working at breakneck speed, I take only four minutes to complete a painting. I'm comfortable I can do it in four minutes because that's what I've trained myself to do.

What was about to happen to me, though, had nothing to do with comfort, and everything to do with pushing myself to the limits—and beyond.

The producers of the wildly popular TV show *America's Got Talent* had booked me to perform on air, and soon we were on the phone going over the particulars. I was told there would be hundreds of people in the studio audience, with millions more watching at home on TV. That was no problem, I assured them—I'd performed before for enormous live crowds and on TV.

I wouldn't just be painting, however; I was going to be judged by a panel of experts. The panel, in fact, was comprised of some very intimidating celebrities, including Howie Mandel, Heidi Klum, Mel B, and Howard Stern. Again, I told the producers—a piece of cake. I had been performing for decades, and had plied my craft in front of many famous people.

"Give me four minutes," I said, "and I'll make magic happen."

"Oh no," the producers told me, "we can't give you four minutes—this is *television*. You have exactly 90 seconds to do your act."

Just 90 seconds!? That was less than half the time I needed to create a terrific speed painting. My process was already stripped down to the bone.

"We're sorry, but 90 seconds is all you'll have," the producers repeated. "Can you do it?"

Despite the risks I'd be taking—including the possibility of failure and public humiliation in front of a television audience of *millions*—there was only one correct answer to the question: "Absolutely!" I said, "I can do it."

The opportunity was too big to pass up. In that split second, I made a decision that had the potential to change my life. I made the decision based not on fear, but on success—I *can* do it and I *will* do it.

In that split second, I decided to head toward the challenge rather than to run away from it.

Heading toward challenges is a skill I've had to master throughout my career. Now it's something I do naturally, almost without thinking. As a result, I soon found myself on stage—looking out at the huge audience and being questioned by the four celebrity judges. With that, Howie Mandel said, "Go for it," and I stepped up to the easel and got to work. In this case, getting to work meant painting a portrait with paintbrushes and clear glue.

Exactly 90 seconds after I began my performance, I threw two big cups of gold glitter at the black canvas and Howard Stern's huge portrait was instantly revealed in all its glory. The audience was blown away by my performance. Stern and the other judges couldn't believe their eyes.

People are just as astonished when I perform as a mentalist and make predictions, foretell future events, and read people's minds. "How did you *do* that?" people ask, "That was *incredible!*"

You might think I have some kind of extraordinary power, but I don't. I've just learned how to tap into the power of split-second success to achieve positive and often dramatic results fast—and so can *you.*

I've been performing for more than 30 years as "The World's Foremost Mentalist" and as a speed and performance painter. I've given thousands of performances for corporations, associations, nonprofits, colleges, and universities. In addition, I run a successful speakers bureau, Power Performers (www.PowerPerformers.com and www.CollegePowerPerformers.com), and I have two websites for my mentalist and speed painting acts (www.RobertChanning.com and www.ImaginationIntoArt.com).

In this book I will share with you my formula for quickly transforming a thought into reality. You'll be introduced to the secrets of split-second decision-making, and I'm going to show you why you should run *toward* challenges instead of running away from them. If you follow the strategies I outline, you, too, will enjoy split-second success—in your business, in your career, and in your life. If you believe you can do it, you can do it—*anything* is possible.

"The will to do comes from the knowledge that we can do."

—JAMES ALLEN, BRITISH AUTHOR

BROKE AND BROKENHEARTED

Although I have had the privilege of making numerous appearances on national network TV—including the *Today* show, the *Steve Harvey Show,* and many others—what I'm most proud of is being hired as a keynote speaker for some of the most successful companies and organizations in the world, including Pepsi, Mercedes-Benz, Walt Disney World, Johnson & Johnson, Yum! Brands, American Express, and many others. My job is to delight and inspire organizations in real time, in a matter of minutes.

I am going to teach you how to create decisive change in your life in an instant.

But before we get started, let me tell you a little about myself....

I grew up in New York. No, not the Big Apple. Not on Broadway. Not even in Brooklyn. In a small town in upstate New York. Before I got too far along in my schooling, it was clear that I had a learning disability. Reading and comprehension was extremely difficult for me. The letters on the page just looked like hieroglyphics, and I couldn't make any sense of them. One day, I overheard my teacher tell my mother that she feared I might never read. While those words might have crushed some kids, it made me want to fight even harder to prove that I was destined for success.

And that's exactly what I did.

> *"[There] can be as much value in the blink of an eye as in months of traditional analysis."*
>
> —Malcolm Gladwell, *Blink*

I made an internal decision to not only learn to read, but to become a *great* reader, and one day even a writer. No one else was aware of this decision, but it didn't matter. I had a new mission in life, and I wasn't going to rest until I achieved my goals. This was my first experience with split-second success, and the lessons I learned from it laid the foundation for the success that followed.

With a lot of hard work, I reached my goal. In a matter of months, I started passing my reading classes, and I showed that teacher how very wrong she was.

Before we go any further, I want to be super clear about something: there's no shortcut to success. It's not like buying a lottery ticket, getting lucky, and winning a million bucks. You've got to put in the time, and you've got to dedicate yourself to greatness. It might take years before all that hard work pays off, but I can guarantee you it will. Luck is where preparation meets opportunity. You can't skip out on doing the work it takes to create your dream life.

And believe me, you'll be challenged, even after you've found the success you're looking for. I've lost loved ones, including one of my precious children. I've had business associates I thought I could trust who have ripped me off.

But guess what? I am a blessed man. I have a beautiful wife, a marvelous family, and a booming career. I have the opportunity to surprise and amaze audiences all around the world, I'm the owner of a successful speakers bureau, and I have become a highly sought-out business thought leader. It has taken me a lot of hard work and dedication to get to where I am today, and it all started with a belief that I am worthy and capable of split-second success.

HERE'S THE KEYNOTE

When I am hired as a keynote speaker—to inspire and motivate a large group of people—my words often set the overarching theme of an entire sales convention or leadership conference. When people thank me after my speech for getting them charged up to make positive changes in their lives, I know I've done my job.

So what is the keynote of this book? What is the core message?

You can create remarkable success in a split second.

I will show you why speed is absolutely critical to your success. More important, I will reveal how you can experience split-second success in your own life, and make it last. Just as in my work as a speed artist and mentalist—where I have learned how to paint masterpieces in minutes and read minds in a split second (in the time it takes you visualize a thought, I've already read your mind)—you will discover how to quickly create new levels of achievement in your own life.

In the pages that follow, I'll show you...

- How to assess any business situation and make the right decision faster than ever
- How to be a "speedster" without getting stressed out
- How to read changes in your markets and competition and turn your organization on a dime
- How to trust your intuition and win big time
- How to build confidence, engagement, and loyalty in your people
- How to finally get past what's been holding you back
- How a single moment of clarity can change everything in your life for the better

This book will touch on business, technology, psychology, spirituality, and the latest research on brain science. But mostly, it's about your success and how to experience it faster. If you read this book with an open mind and complete the Fast Action Steps exercises at the end of each chapter, I absolutely promise that...

- You'll gain more of what you want—in your business, career, and life.
- You'll achieve the successes you've been dreaming of faster than ever before.
- You'll exchange your feelings of self-doubt for self-confidence.

Warning

I'm going to show you some powerful techniques for getting exactly what you've been hoping for—faster than you ever thought possible. Please do *not* use the strategies in this book to accomplish anything that is illegal, immoral, or that would be an embarrassment to your grandmother. I invite you to use these powerful techniques (and your own powers) for good.

Three more things before we get started.

1. You can read this book in any sequence you like, but I recommend you read it in order, from chapter 1 to chapter 10, and then the afterword. Why? Because the strategies contained in each chapter build on the concepts taught in the previous chapter.
2. Do the Fast Action Steps exercises at the end of each chapter *immediately* after you finish reading it. And be sure to write down your biggest takeaway. Like any important transaction or agreement in your life—such as getting a good price on the house of your dreams or signing the paperwork to adopt a child—you need to *get it in writing.*
3. Read the book *fast!* You can go back and read it again, but your best results will come from taking just enough time to understand the concepts, and then to put them into action. As the Nike ads used to say, *just do it!*

It's truly an honor for me to be your guide as you journey toward a life of creating positive results for yourself and others. I'm thrilled to help you move from being boxed in by the self-imposed boundaries and limits in your life to the exhilarating freedom and satisfaction of split-second success. Every word in this book comes from the heart, and it lands on the heart.

I hope you'll take time to tell me about your own split-second success stories. I look forward to reading them.

So, now…

Let's. Get. Going.

—Robert Channing, New York

CHAPTER 1

FAST = FABULOUS

"Change the story you've been telling yourself about what is possible. Create a narrative where you succeed so fast that you amaze everybody around you, and blow your own mind too."

—RUBEN PADILLA, THE NARRATIVE STRATEGIST

THE PURPOSE OF this first chapter is simple: I want to be sure you realize that fast is fabulous. Before we get into the *hows* of super-speedy success, let's first take a moment and reflect on the *wows* of rapid results. We live in a culture where speed is often synonymous with success—the faster we can make a decision and act on an opportunity, the better the chances that we will beat our competition to the punch. We *love* things that go fast.

AND THEY'RE OFF

Take horse racing, for example. In 2015, a horse won the famous Triple Crown for the first time in 37 years. His name was American Pharoah, and the sporting world went nuts over his win. I'm sure you're familiar with the expression, "He won by a nose." But here's something you might not know related to horse racing: When a horse wins a race but is faster by only a second—or even just one-tenth of a second—that horse wins a cash prize that's 10 times bigger than the prize won by the horse that comes in second.

While the winning horse is nowhere near 10 times faster than the second-place finisher, we love to reward horses, and humans, who get across the finish line the fastest. Before he won the Triple Crown, American Pharoah's stud value—the amount he might earn from breeding—was $20 million, not exactly chicken feed. However, after he won the Triple Crown, the horse's stud value shot up to an estimated $100 million.

Winning horses are prized because they are the *fastest*, not because they are the friendliest, the strongest, the nicest, the happiest, or the most attractive.

Speed wins, every day of the week.

Does anyone remember the name of the horse that came in second to American Pharoah in any of the three big races? Odds are good the answer is no. Second-place finishers are often quickly forgotten, even if the second-place horse came in just a split second behind.

"The race may not always be to the swift
nor the victory to the strong, but that's how you bet."

—HUGH E. KEOUGH, CHICAGO SPORTSWRITER

The concept of speed being equal to success isn't true just in sports; it's true in business, too. Remember the bookstore chain Borders? As the nation's second-largest bookstore, it used to be in just about every shopping mall in America. But Amazon crushed Borders by offering a better selection and speedy delivery. Book buyers liked being able to browse the virtual shelves of Amazon without having to jump into their cars to do it. Not only did they love the convenience, they loved the prices, which across the board were better than those offered by the brick-and-mortar book retailers. Borders went out of business in 2011.

And remember Blockbuster? Their stores used to be in every town in America. But Netflix made the video-rental company nearly obsolete by focusing on what customers want: movies *now*.

Abraham Lincoln's masterpiece, the Gettysburg Address, is known for being short and powerful. At just 272 words, it took Lincoln only two minutes to deliver, but his message of hope and American ideals has guided our nation for more than 150 years. A man named Edward Everett also gave a speech that day, at the dedication of the Gettysburg National Cemetery. His speech lasted two hours and ran more than 13,000 words, but I doubt a single American today has any idea what he said, or even who Edward Everett was. To have a lasting impact, you have to get right to the point.

Your Mind Is Racing Too

Ever hear someone say, "My mind is going a mile a minute?" That rate works out to 60 mph. A mile a minute may seem fast, but by today's standards, it's not fast enough. In this age of instant information, split-second thinking is critical to your success. On top of that, you need to direct your thinking in very specific ways. You need a finish line, a goal, an end zone, a target. I'll talk more about this in coming chapters to help you create rapid results.

You're probably familiar with the phrase YOLO, which is an acronym for "You only live once." While it's a great reminder of why seizing the day is important for any of us, I think LISS! is even more important for most of us. It stands for "Life is super short!" Even if you live to the ripe old age of 112, that's just the blink of an eye compared to the time that humans have walked the Earth. Our lives happen fast—they fly by in an instant. As you look back on your life, what do you cherish the most? Most likely, it's the special moments and snapshots in time: your daughter's first steps, your first kiss, getting your first promotion at work, or crossing the finish line of your first marathon.

You can create more moments to treasure by thinking and acting fast.

By "fast," "rapid," and "quick," I don't mean you need to become busier than you already are. Sometimes all it takes is a little push to create real change. And more often than not, that energy for the push already exists within you. You just need to harness it for the right purposes.

Life Is Mind-Blowing

With my mentalist and speed-painting performances, I'm in the business of blowing people's minds. Each time I take the stage I perform wonders that amaze and dazzle the members of my audience—and it's truly a wonderful feeling. I turn skeptics into believers, and doubters into fans. Believe me, it's a feeling that never gets old. But one thing I've learned is that the most amazing thing of all is life itself. And I'm not alone in this realization.

In 2005, Steve Jobs gave the commencement speech to the graduating students at Stanford University. Less than a year before his speech, Jobs revealed to the world that he was suffering from a rare form of pancreatic cancer. In his speech, Jobs drove home how important it is to take advantage of the short time each of us has on this planet we call Earth.

> *When I was 17, I read a quote that went something like: "If you live each day as if it was your last, someday you'll most certainly be right." It made an impression on me, and since then, for the past 33 years, I have looked in the mirror every morning and asked myself: "If today were the last day of my life, would I want to do what I am about to do today?" And whenever the answer has been "No" for too many days in a row, I know I need to change something.*

What is most amazing about Jobs's story is not that he faced death that day; others have faced the same destiny. What makes the moment incredible is his profound realization that every day is a gift. Every day that you wake up is like a reprieve; you are given a brand-new chance to live a successful and happy life. Though Steve Jobs's epiphany was especially dramatic, he is not the only person to have a split-second breakthrough.

10 Cents Turned into 10 Million Copies

"Stuff your eyes with wonder…live as if you'd drop dead in 10 seconds."

—Ray Bradbury, *Fahrenheit 451*

Ray Bradbury never went before a firing squad, but he had a unique way of using the pressure of speed to get himself fired up to write. He used what I call a *split-second success mechanism* to create his masterpiece *Fahrenheit 451*. The book has sold more than 10 million copies and been translated into more than 30 languages. What was Bradbury's secret success mechanism? He forced himself to create—and to create *fast*.

But before there was the bestselling book, there was a short story he wrote for *Galaxy Science Fiction* magazine titled "The Fireman." Bradbury had a wife and two children at home, and he was desperate to find a quiet place to write. While working in the UCLA Library, he followed the sound of clacking keys to a room in the basement, which had 12 typewriters available for rent at 10 cents a half-hour. After time ran out, you had to drop in another dime. Needless to say, it was in your best interest to type as quickly as you could.

Soon, Bradbury discovered that forcing himself to write in 30-minute bursts was a giant game-changer. He found himself enjoying the work—pumping out material quickly, and then taking occasional breaks. His creativity flowed because there wasn't time for him to doubt his work. He just did it.

Nine days later, after dropping $9.80 worth of dimes into the UCLA library typewriters, Bradbury had banged out the 60 pages he needed to finish "The Fireman." He later expanded the story into *Fahrenheit 451*—returning to the basement of the UCLA library to complete the task in just nine days.

Soon after the book was published, Groff Conklin, a science fiction anthologist and critic for *Galaxy Science Fiction*, said it was "among the great works of imagination written in English in the last decade or more." Today, Bradbury's novel has been turned into a play, a radio drama, a graphic novel, and even a computer video game. Remarkably, Bradbury's success was triggered when he was forced to type quickly as the timer counted down the minutes.

Are you ready for *your* breakthrough? Would you like to achieve and feel the way you want to *right now*? In the next chapter, I'll provide you with a method for creating magical results right on the spot. But for now, give these fast action steps a try. Don't overthink it—just do it!

> *"Split-second success is a split-second decision;*
> *it's all the agonizing that takes so much time."*

— ROBERT CHANNING

FAST ACTION STEPS

1. Think back to a time when you had to think or act fast and the result was fantastic. How did you do it? Write down this experience.
2. Have you ever experienced a breakthrough insight? What was that realization? Write it down. Have you cherished it enough? Why is this idea so powerful for you?
3. When have you experienced a burst of motivation—at work, in sports, or in life—when an increase in speed or effectiveness had a massive impact on your health, wealth, or happiness? Write down that moment and how it felt.
4. Where in your life do you feel slow or stuck? What can you do to change your flow from a slow to a fast setting? How can you force yourself into a more productive environment or routine?
5. What type of split-second success inspires you most? Racecar driving? The rise of Bitcoin technology? Olympic sprinters? How can you model what your speed heroes have accomplished, and apply it to your work?

CHAPTER 2

How to Think Fast

"Thought is the original source of all wealth, all success."

—CLAUDE BRISTOL, *THE MAGIC OF BELIEVING*

THINKING IS THE first step to success. Thinking faster will help you succeed sooner. And I have great news for you: No matter who you are, you have the ability to accelerate your thinking and your achievements.

I make my living thinking fast and acting now in front of large, live audiences. Today, I am a successful keynote speaker, a master mentalist, and the world's fastest speed painter. But I wasn't always so confident. I used to be afraid. I used to live in a self-made world of doubt and procrastination. However, that all changed for me in 1988.

It's About Time

1988 was the year I booked my first big gig—$900 to do my 45-minute mentalism show for the largest community college in the state of New York. Nine hundred dollars! For me—a young man living at his parents' house—that was a fortune. And it all began as a simple thought: *I want to perform for the students of Mohawk Valley Community College and get paid for it.*

But I didn't just end with a thought, with a wish and a prayer; I followed the thought with action. I made a cold call to the student activities chairperson at Mohawk Valley, describing the show I would put on, which would include mindreading and hypnosis. I told him that if he hired me, I would mail him a sealed letter with a prediction of what he and his fellow committee members would be wearing the night I performed. We would open the letter live on stage and see if I was right. Intrigued, he immediately booked me for the $900 I asked for. I was so excited that I did a handstand on my mom's chair and accidentally kicked a hole in the ceiling. Then I mailed that guy a sealed envelope with my fashion prediction.

A month later I was on my way to Mohawk Valley to perform. I had been honing my skills in small venues, and I knew I was ready. As I took the stage I was confident that I was about to blow the students' minds, and, as I predicted, the show was a huge success. As promised, when the event committee members walked on stage and opened the sealed envelope I had sent them the month before, they were wearing exactly what I had predicted—right down to the color of their socks and the stripes on their shirts. (How did I do that? Nice try, but a professional never reveals his secrets!) I floated home on cloud nine, only coming down long enough to give my parents $50 to repair the hole in their ceiling.

This life-altering experience taught me the two-pronged secret of split-second success. First, you need a specific, clear, and promising thought that you truly believe in. And, second, you need to act on that thought *immediately*. No excuses. No procrastinating. No putting it off until tomorrow. I had the clear thought in my mind that I wanted to perform at the Mohawk Valley Community College. And then, instead of talking myself out of it and giving in to my self-doubt—*You're too young. You're not ready yet. They don't know you. You've never done this*—I believed I could do it and I *took action*. I made the call and booked the gig.

That first big event led to many others. For more than 25 years, I have made my living as a performer, which means I live and die by booking jobs. If I don't get booked, my kids don't eat. Getting paid to give live presentations in a highly competitive arena requires me to think quickly, both on stage and off.

THINKING ON YOUR FEET

I love the story of the motivational speaker who only had a split second to salvage a booking he was about to lose. A corporate event planner asked him, "How much do you charge for a keynote program?" As a newbie he hemmed and hawed.

"Um…it depends. Let's see. Uh…."

She interrupted him, "How much?"

"I charge $1,500," he blurted out.

The meeting planner was accustomed to spending far more than that for her programs. "Oh, this may not be the right fit for us," she said. "Last year we spent $10,000 on our guest speaker."

The motivational speaker thought quickly and changed gears. "Fifteen-hundred is the deposit. My full fee is $12,000."

He got the gig.

HOW TO THINK ON THE SPOT

There is an amazing strategy for developing this kind of quick thinking. It uses the simple acronym SPOT, which stands for *Show Up, Perceive, Overcome, and Take Action*. I guarantee that this strategy will help you think faster, simplify your decision-making, and bring you success sooner than you ever imagined. In fact, I wish I had learned this principle years ago—it would have saved me a lot of time, money, and energy that I wasted on slow thinking and procrastination.

THE SPOT STRATEGY

SHOW UP

Let's say you have a problem to solve, an opportunity to consider, or a decision to make. The first step is to be fully present in your body, and in the time, place, and surroundings in which you find yourself. In his marvelous book, *Four Seconds: All the Time You Need to Stop Counter-Productive Habits and Get the Results You Want,* Peter Bregman teaches that it takes just four seconds to do the one thing that changes everything.

What is that one thing?

Breathe!

Take a good deep breath into your lungs. It's energizing to your body, and it recharges your brain so you can concentrate.

"You never open your mouth until you know what the shot is."

—AL PACINO AS RICKY ROMA IN *GLENNGARY GLEN ROSS*

PERCEIVE

Awareness is essential for thinking fast. Tap into your senses of sight, hearing, smell, and instinct, and intuitively size-up the situation. What do you want? What is the problem? Who will be affected by the outcome? What is the opportunity here? Listen to your gut feeling. Trust yourself.

Two things will happen. First, you'll have a powerful idea. Second, a wave of doubt, fear, or self-criticism will wash over you, which is why you need the next step.

OVERCOME

Don't ignore the negative reactions that rise up inside you—the anxiety, fear, and nervousness. If you do, these emotions will crush you. Instead, face them, acknowledge them, and then quickly get back to your original idea. Seize that first thought, that higher impulse: *I know what to do.*

TAKE ACTION

Remember the classic children's story, *The Little Engine That Could?* The determined, little train engine had a winning thought and he repeated it out loud: "I think I can. I think I can. I think I can." But the engine also *did* something with this thought—*he started moving.* He got rolling.

The Little Engine thought he could and then did what it took to turn his thought into the success that he imagined in his mind.

Use this as a reminder. Take immediate action when you have a powerful thought that you believe will lead you to your desired goal.

By applying SPOT thinking to the next problem, decision or challenge you face, you'll quickly create more winning results. Why not try it right now? Apply SPOT thinking as you work through the questions in the Fast Action Steps that follow. Jot down your answers—*fast!*

Fast Action Steps

1. Write about a time when you had a crystal-clear thought that you took immediate action on. What was the thought? What happened? How did you make it happen?
2. Think of a situation in which you feel bogged down. What are you avoiding thinking about? What are you procrastinating doing? Take five minutes and put this challenging situation through the SPOT sequence: Show up—*breathe.* What do you perceive? What feeling will you overcome? How will you take action?
3. What is the *one thing* you know you must *do* right now to tackle that challenging situation? What steps will you take to get that action rolling immediately—right *now?*
4. What can you think fast about that could create the biggest positive change in your life? Now, take action and make it happen. You can do it!

CHAPTER 3

FAST DESTROYS FEAR

"If you hear a voice within you say, 'You cannot paint,'
then by all means paint, and that voice will be silenced."

—VINCENT VAN GOGH

FEAR IS ONE of the biggest hurdles you must overcome to be successful. But you *can* conquer your fears. And the faster you face your fears with swift and decisive action, the sooner you will enjoy split-second success.

By itself, fear isn't necessarily a bad thing. It's a natural biological response (the "fight-or-flight" reaction) when we sense there's danger in the air. Fear releases powerful hormones into our bloodstream that get our minds and bodies activated and ready to do something quick (like run away as fast as we can from that charging grizzly bear) if that danger turns out to be real. The problem with fear is that it can get in the way of achieving our goals when we let it get the better of us.

You've probably shared the same fear that many of us have—public speaking. Many of us start sweating and shaking at just the thought of standing on a stage in front of a couple hundred people, much less actually doing it. According to researchers, public speaking beats out the fear of death as the number one fear in America. Sadly, unwarranted fears such as these can stop us from achieving the success we want in our lives.

In modern society, people have different ideas about what fear means. Many different four-word phrases using FEAR as an acronym have been created to capture the meaning of the word. Here are some of my favorites:

- FEAR = False Emotions Appearing Real
- FEAR = Forget Everything and Run
- FEAR = Future Events Already Ruined
- FEAR = Failure Expected and Received

Notice how each one of these phrases is based on negative thinking—on the assumption that things are going to go terribly bad for us. So, what happens when we re-paint the acronym FEAR in a positive light?

- FEAR = Feeling Excited and Ready

Or, my all-time favorite:

- FEAR = Face Everything and Rise!

Make fear your friend. Instead of running away from the things you fear, run *to* them. When it comes to fear, the key is not what you *think* about it, it's what you *do* about it. And to truly conquer your fears, the important thing is what you do about it right *now*.

Want your fears to shrink or disappear fast? Then *act fast.*

"Find out what you're afraid of and go live there."

—CHUCK PALAHNIUK, *INVISIBLE MONSTERS*

Let me give you an everyday example. Let's say you have a young son or daughter who needs a Band-Aid removed from his or her knee. What are you going to do? Will you give a pep talk about it? Will you encourage him to think new thoughts about it? Will you tell her to pull off the Band-Aid S-L-O-W-L-Y? I doubt it. You'll probably do what I do.

I am the father of four children and speed is my best friend. So I put my arm around my son or daughter and then WHAP! I pull the Band-Aid off in an instant. Yes, it hurts, but just for a second or two. And they are quickly out of the agony of thinking and worrying about what's coming—dreading the pain they imagine they will feel, and avoiding what must be done. My method may not be fun for me or my kids, but it is effective. It moves them past their fear quickly so they can get on with their day.

When facing your fears, do what needs to be done *quickly*. It will move you a giant step closer to your split-second success.

ACTION DESTROYS FEAR

Ryan Penneau is a dynamic trainer and success mentor to thousands of college students. According to Ryan, the fastest way to erase fear is to follow these six simple, but powerful steps:

Step 1: Get out of your head
Step 2: Get into your heart
Step 3: Get an accountability buddy
Step 4: Think abundance, not scarcity
Step 5: Trust yourself
Step 6: Take action

"Fear?" Penneau tells students, "This too shall pass. I urge you to constantly, passionately, and incessantly remind yourself that discomfort, fear, and pain are only temporary. You will get over it. Just like you got over that thing from 10 years ago."

When one of his students asks, "What thing?" he replies, "See? You don't even remember it now."

When you put off dealing with your fears, you make them worse. Your mind will actually magnify your fears. What you resist will persist.

Penneau suggests you change your thinking from, "What if this goes badly?" to "When this works, it will be awesome!"

One of the main takeaways from Penneau's work regarding fear is this: You *are* mentally and physically capable of jumping into and through your fears. What stops you is your emotions. So when you feel those emotional triggers coming on, *do* something about them. Change your environment. Say something different. Make a sandwich or make a phone call. Stand in a different room. Take action!

> *"Feel the fear.*
> *And do it anyway."*

—SUSAN JEFFERS, BEST-SELLING SELF-HELP AUTHOR

FLEX YOUR SUCCESS MUSCLES

Even athletes agree: Action destroys fear.

You might remember basketball great Michael Jordan's commercial for Nike, where he made his fear a badge of honor. As Michael steps out of a limo and walks into the basketball arena, you hear his sober voice recount the failures he has faced in his career: "I've missed more than 9,000 shots in my career. I've lost almost 300 games. Twenty-six times, I've been trusted to take the winning shot and missed. I've failed over and over again in my life. And that is why I succeed."

As hockey legend Wayne Gretzky put it, "You miss one hundred percent of the shots you don't take." No matter how much fear you feel, you've got to keep taking those shots, keep moving forward.

Every athlete suffers from periods of poor performance, known as slumps. But immediate and persistent action helps them get out of those slumps. It's all thanks to something called muscle memory. When you do something right over and over again—make a three-point shot in basketball, hit a homerun in baseball, or drive the ball far and true down the fairway in golf, your muscles will "remember" what success feels like and they will be able to recreate that action automatically. These wins eliminate the fear and anxiety of poor performance and lift athletes out of their slump.

Muscle memory can also help you overcome the fear of making decisions. Like your muscles, the brain remembers what success feels like and it can learn to recreate that success automatically. It all starts with action. Begin by making small decisions that lead to small successes—making a sale, losing a pound or two, or making 25 new connections on your LinkedIn or Twitter page—and then replicate those decisions on a larger scale or in other areas of your life. Once you've established a pattern of positive outcomes stemming from the decisions you've made, you'll gain confidence and decisions will become easier and faster. So will your success. Besides, when you face your fear with action, you're in good company. It's exactly what heroes do.

BECOME THE HERO OF YOUR OWN MOVIE

Nearly all the blockbuster movie scripts of the last 40 years—including *Star Wars, The Lord of the Rings* and *The Hunger Games*—are built around something known as "the hero's journey." According to American mythologist Joseph Campbell, the hero's journey is about the journey each of us must take to face our fears as we follow our path toward our own destiny. Campbell put it this way:

"The cave you fear to enter holds the treasure you seek."

—JOSEPH CAMPBELL

One of the highest-paid action movie heroes today is Dwayne "The Rock" Johnson. On his way to fame and fortune, he had to take action after action to break through his fears. According to The Rock, it was quite a journey.

"In '95, I had seven bucks," he once said. "By '96, I was wrestling in flea markets for 40 bucks a night."

In 2013—less than 20 years after he was just seven bucks away from being completely broke—The Rock was ranked #1 on the Forbes list of top-grossing actors.

"Some of you out there might be going through your own 'seven bucks in your pocket' situation," he says. "Embrace the grind, lower your shoulder, and keep drivin' through."

Notice that The Rock says, "drivin' *through*." Fear is not something you get over or around. Fear is what heroes must go *through* to get what they really want.

Seek Out What You Are Afraid Of

Why not take this idea one step deeper and actually go after the things you are afraid of?

You might think that a brilliant genius like Albert Einstein would have little to fear, but this was definitely not the case. For years, Albert Einstein actively lobbied for peace in Europe, giving speeches, attending press conferences, and joining the German League for Human Rights, which pushed for disarmament of the major powers. However, at the same time, Einstein's activities in support of peace began to attract the attention of the supporters of Adolph Hitler, who was fast gaining in influence and power, within Germany's borders, and beyond.

Although Einstein's friends told him that he should keep his head down, and avoid confronting this rising menace, he refused. No matter the consequences to himself, he wouldn't allow the Nazis to rise to power unchallenged. Soon after Hitler became Chancellor of Germany on January 30, 1933, Nazi officials confiscated Einstein's property in Germany. This act devastated Einstein, but he continued to speak out against the regime. "A group of armed bandits," he said, "has successfully silenced the responsible sections of the population and imposed a kind of revolution from below which will soon destroy or paralyze everything that is civilized."

While Einstein was unable to stop the rise of Adolph Hitler and the Nazis, he spoke out against them at every opportunity. He did not allow fear to rule his life, or to dissuade him from his path in life.

Remember: Do the thing you fear *now*, and your fear will soon be gone. It will be replaced with split-second success.

FAST ACTION STEPS

1. What are you afraid of today? Be super specific.
2. What would happen if you were on the other side of that fear?
3. What one action (for example, a phone call, a difficult conversation, a new discipline, an apology) can you take right now that will move you in the direction of freedom from fear?
4. What do you need to face in your life so you can find the treasure you are seeking?
5. Who do you have in your life who can support you as you face your fears?
6. How can you get into high gear to beat your fears? What *fast actions* can you take to make your fear dissolve even faster?

CHAPTER 4

TURNING YOUR THOUGHTS INTO THINGS

"Whatever the mind can conceive and believe, it can achieve."

—NAPOLEON HILL, *THINK AND GROW RICH*

THE MORNING AFTER my speed-painting appearance on *The Steve Harvey Show*, one of my neighbors rushed up to me outside my house. He asked me the same thing I have been asked by thousands of people following my performances: "I saw you create that painting in a matter of seconds! How did you do that? Is there some kind of trick to it?"

My secret is so simple, it just might surprise you.

IT'S AS EASY AS 1, 2, 3

My formula for painting "a masterpiece in minutes" relies on the same strategy I use when I perform my mind-reading act, when I buy a home, or when I start a new business. I even used this approach subconsciously to find and marry the woman of my dreams—and we are still happily married today.

Here's what I do when I take my thoughts and quickly transform them into works of art.

1. **I SEE** a picture in my imagination of what I want to create.
2. **I BELIEVE** in my heart of hearts that I will create it.
3. **I DO IT** by taking immediate action.

I'm an artist, but people think I'm some kind of rare genius. The truth is you can learn to do what I do. You can create things that are meaningful to you—and you can do it *fast*.

I learned this sequence for turning thoughts into reality from the master success teacher Napoleon Hill. No other success teacher has had a bigger impact on the personal growth movement in the last 100 years than Hill. His 1937 book, *Think and Grow Rich*, is quickly approaching the mark of 100 million copies sold worldwide.

"King of the Hill" is how I think of him. Hill wrote thousands of pages about his laws of success, but he may have summed it up in a single statement—the quotation at the top of this chapter. I am going to share it with you again because I want you to install this principle deep into your heart and mind. It's extremely potent. Hill said:

Whatever the mind can conceive and believe, it can achieve.

Now notice how my three secret steps for turning imagination into art are based on Hill's great success formula. I merely put the steps into my own words. You can translate Napoleon Hill's idea into your own words, too. Before every performance, I say it to myself like this…

SEE IT. BELIEVE IT. DO IT.

You can model this principle in your own life. As motivational speaker Tony Robbins teaches, "Success leaves clues." Watch and learn from other achievers doing what you want to do. Just as I modeled my fast-creation formula on Hill's main idea, Hill himself was influenced by the ideas of another master mentor.

HILL HAD TO MAKE A SPLIT-SECOND DECISION

Though he worked tirelessly for many years, Hill explained that his entire philosophy of personal achievement was birthed in a moment. He took just 29 seconds to make a monumental decision that would transform his life and the lives of countless others.

Here's how he says it happened.

Hill, at that time a young reporter, was assigned to interview Andrew Carnegie as part of a series on famous, powerful men. Carnegie, who was the Bill Gates of his day, created an enormous steel empire that made him a self-made mega-success and the richest man in America. Hill may have expected a typical interview—but he was in for a big surprise.

Carnegie granted Hill an interview, but also offered him something more. He told Hill that if he was serious about learning the secrets of success, Carnegie would introduce him to the most accomplished men in the world, giving Hill an insider's look into the thinking and habits of men who were massive successes.

Carnegie asked Hill whether he was willing to work tirelessly on the project—for 20 years. He offered Hill no money, but was willing to open doors for him if the young man would document what he learned, turn it into a philosophy of success, and share it with the world.

At the very moment Carnegie offered his invitation to Hill, he secretly punched a stopwatch hidden beneath his desk. Carnegie had learned that super-successful people make decisions quickly and act on them immediately. Had Hill not given him an answer within 60 seconds, Carnegie would have dismissed him.

Hill said it took him just 29 seconds to say, "Yes," and the rest is history.

Hill seized the opportunity. He saw himself as the man who would teach the world about a concrete system for success. He intensely believed this was his destiny. And he did it. Hill became the dean of American success, and his words burn just as brightly today as they did decades ago. Quickly accepting Carnegie's invitation reshaped Hill's entire life and planted in his mind a burning purpose that he ultimately turned into reality.

THINK ON PURPOSE

By now, you may find your inner critic saying, "Well, I'm no Napoleon Hill. And I'm certainly no Andrew Carnegie..."

Stop right there.

You are a human, just like them. And you already bring your thoughts into reality every day, just as these men did.

Take a look around. You continually bring about what you think about. Look at your clothes—you *thought* about what you would wear today. You *believed* you would look and feel your best wearing them. And then you *took action*—you put them on.

And why are you reading this book? Because you *think* it will help you. And guess what? Reading this book *will* help you.

See my point? You can't help but think about something, and you can't help but turn that something into reality.

The real question is this: *Are you thinking on purpose?*

You have the freedom to choose what to think about. So get ready to think hard (and fast) about what you want. And train your brain to *think on purpose*.

STATE WHAT YOU WANT TO CREATE

More than 40 million people from all around the world have followed the advice of success guru Tony Robbins to turn their dreams into reality. According to Robbins, there are three steps for creating an extraordinary life. Ask yourself these questions and listen—really listen—to the answers you hear in your mind.

Step 1: What do you really want?
Step 2: What's preventing you from having it?
Step 3: How do you change your life now?

As you can see, everything starts with Step 1: What do you really want? To unleash the remarkable power within you, you've got to figure out exactly what it is that you want to create, and then state it clearly so you understand it fully. Write it down, and then hone it into the goal that reflects your deepest desires.

*"There is a powerful driving force inside ev-
ery human being that, once unleashed, can make
any vision, dream, or desire a reality."*

—TONY ROBBINS, BEST-SELLING AUTHOR
AND MOTIVATIONAL SPEAKER

When a painter creates a work of art, he is simply putting a line around his thoughts. And just as an artist pictures what he wants to create and then creates it, you can imagine what you want and create it for yourself. The old saying is true: *What you see is what you get.*

SEE FOR YOURSELF

One of the most dramatic parts of my keynote message and mentalist performance happens when I can't see anything at all. Two large coins, a bunch of tape, and a blindfold cover my eyes—three layers ensure I will not be able to depend on my sense of sight. Yet I am able to describe in detail the clothes that people in the audience are wearing, the serial numbers on their dollar bills, and much more.

Many people want to know how I do it—which, again, I'm not going to reveal. A professional performer never tells. But I will tell you *why* I do it, which is far more powerful. I'm driven to do it because I want to demonstrate that human beings can use their knowledge, intuition, and imagination to immediately create stunning results. The good news is that you can, too.

*"Imagination is the beginning of creation.
You imagine what you desire;*

you will what you imagine;
and at last you create what you will."

—GEORGE BERNARD SHAW, IRISH PLAYWRIGHT

I'm a speed painter, but you may not own a paintbrush or have any interest in painting at all. That's okay—you can still "brush with greatness." It starts with your imagination. That's where every great invention, new product, breakthrough technology, and scientific advance begins. But it doesn't end there.

Let me expand on the flow of my three-part sequence for turning thoughts into things.

It looks like this:

- Picture what you want. Be vivid with your imagination. Your mind thinks in pictures, so get your picture in focus.
- Zoom in on exactly what it looks like. See the color, size, and shape of what you want to create.
- Permit yourself to have it. It's easier when you remember *why* you want it.
- Passionately want what you want. Crank up the actual feelings that are fueling your thought. *The language of your heart is emotional.*
- Plan for what you are about to create. Set the table for your success. For me, this means setting up my canvas, paints, and brushes. What is *your* setup?
- Pretend that you have already created it. This goes back to the power of your belief.
- Prioritize *doing* what you need to do to create what you want.

Flash Forward

"Deep within the Flash himself, incredible new powers are ready to be unleashed—unforeseen, unexplored abilities fueled by the same Speed Force that makes the Flash run..."

—Francis Manapul and Brian Buccellato,
The Flash: Move Forward

I want to end this chapter with some thoughts about one of my favorite superheroes: The Flash. (I'm hoping my son will forgive me for not talking about Iron Man, *his* favorite superhero.)

The Flash was born one day when Barry Allen, a guy who worked as a Central City police scientist, was doused in chemicals and struck by a bolt of lightning. This event transformed his life from scientist to superhero—in a split second, Allen became The Flash. But to use his new abilities to their highest level, Allen had to believe he was more than just a regular guy. He had to (literally) run with this new identity.

So do you.

Thought + Belief + Action—that's the secret sauce that will turn your dreams into reality every time.

Become Your Own Superhero

You can become the superhero of your own life. It starts by thinking lightning-bolt fast, believing in your idea, and running fast *toward* what you must do next. You may not become quite as fast as Barry Allen, but you will flash forward into achievements that will thrill you—and amaze your friends and colleagues.

Try it. Think fast, and complete these steps now.

Fast Action Steps

1. What is your personal lightning-bolt realization? What is the thought you want to turn into reality? State what you want to create.
2. Do you really believe in the purpose of your goals? If not, ask yourself the big *why* question. Why do you want to create that? What would it do for you—and for others?
3. What do you need to do right now to create what you want? What is the first step? When will you take it?
4. Do you have a mentor in your life? (This could also be a historical, mythological, or spiritual person you know through reading or study.) What assistance can this mentor give you? What will you do for others in return for this inspiration or help?

CHAPTER 5

How to Act Fast and Create Positive Results Now

"Don't merely dream—but create!"

—Dr. Maxwell Maltz, inventor of Psycho-Cybernetics

Success can come to you in a split second—in the time it takes to say, "Yes."

One morning I got a call from the *Today* show inviting me to be on their program the day after Christmas. As I thought about logistics, I realized that to get to their studio in New York City on time, I'd have to leave my family on Christmas night. I have four kids, and Christmas is a big deal around our house. This was not an easy decision.

I quickly weighed the pros and cons, however, and decided to take the gig.

When the appointed day came, I made the trip, got to the studio, and speed painted the three hosts in a matter of seconds. They loved my performance, and said it was the best segment they had done that entire year. In fact, they loved it so much that NBC expanded my efforts into a one-hour, feature segment.

Amazing things happened after the show aired: Almost overnight I received numerous bookings from big-name celebrities, companies, and even a well-known billionaire. All because I quickly assessed the situation and made a fast decision. I didn't tell the producers I would think about it and get back to them soon.

I thought, I decided, and I acted—while the opportunity was waiting there for me to take.

You can learn to act fast and expedite your success too.

In this chapter I'm going to give you nine strategies that will help you get where you want to go sooner than you ever thought possible.

Strategy 1: Get up early to get the upper hand

There are countless stories of armies that woke up before dawn to launch a sneak attack on their enemies. Their early-bird efforts often resulted in victory. They might have given up a little sleep, but they survived and succeeded in their missions.

Your stakes are probably not as high as the armies mentioned in these stories, but if you begin your day *before* your competitors, you, too, will have the upper hand.

What would happen if you started your day even 20 minutes earlier? How many more sales calls could you add to your week, your month, and your year this way? How many projects could you work on proactively (instead of reactively)? The best use of your early time might be to meditate to get yourself centered or to go to the gym to energize your day. Tap into your inner clock and discover what works best for you.

Acting *first* is one of the secrets to succeeding *fast*. Even sprinters who are slower than their competition can cross the finish line first when they are the first to get out of the starting blocks. So, for a head start, get out of bed sooner.

Strategy 2: Do the things you fear first

Do you have trouble getting things going when you sit down at your desk each morning? According to Alok Bhardwaj, founder of the software startup Hidden Reflex, doing the *worst tasks first* is the best way to start your day. Bhardwaj maintains that if you begin each workday with the least desirable item on your to-do list, it will increase your productivity for the rest of the day.

Try it. When you begin your workday, don't jump into your emails or spend time surfing the Web—instead, get started on the tasks you're dreading most. Make the call you've been putting off to that unhappy client. Schedule that meeting you've been avoiding with all your department heads. Take on that complex spreadsheet or business plan.

You'll feel energized and accomplished after tackling the worst thing first; the task you were avoiding is now behind you. The rest of your day will suddenly look bright, and you'll be able to dive into your responsibilities with energy and enthusiasm. Your newfound positive attitude will help you leap into action, creating the momentum you need be effective and efficient in all of your remaining tasks. You'll also be more pleasant to be around, which could help your teammates have a more productive day, too.

Strategy 3: Create an action environment

As we saw in the section above, doing feared things first is a great way to create an action environment for you *and* your team. To create your own personal action environment, you also need to be in tune with what works for you, and the place where it works best.

Are you better able to focus in a quiet room or in a busy office? Are you more creative when you sit alone at your desk or when you interact with others? Are you more likely to stay committed to working out if you join a jogging group or if you install a home gym?

You also need to be clear about what it is you are trying to accomplish. The perfect action environment for getting your car repaired is probably not the best environment for meeting suppliers to discuss your account. Your productivity will soar when you immerse yourself in the action environment that is ideal for you.

The following story captures this concept in a funny way.

A man hires his hillbilly cousins to paint the fences around his pasture. He sets them up with brushes and rollers and a big bucket of paint, and puts everything near the fence before going off to the far side of the farm to work.

When he returns, his workers have painted an impressive 500 feet of fence. "Great job, cousins," he says.

On day two, he returns to find only 200 more feet of fence painted—not bad, but not nearly as good as on the previous day. "Looks okay, cousins," he says.

On day three, he returns to find only an additional 10 feet of fence painted. "What happened, cousins? On day one, you painted 500 feet, the next day 200, and today almost nothing!"

"Well," one of the cousins replies. "It's a long way back to that paint bucket."

Moving your bucket may be all it takes to create your ideal action environment and experience rapid results.

STRATEGY 4: DO YOUR HOMEWORK

You will waste precious time and energy if you begin your project with the wrong premise, or from the wrong starting line, or facing the wrong direction. An architect who designs a gorgeous two-story home for a client in record time would be seriously behind schedule if what the client wanted was a one-story ranch.

Getting all the facts will help you identify the action that will move your project forward fast. The time you invest in research can pay big dividends at the end.

Take chess, for example: Chess is a notoriously slow game if you don't know how the pieces move. Once you know the patterns, though, you can play "blitz chess" in five-minute, action-packed games.

The key is knowing as much as you can about the game at hand. One correct move might be all you need to win the game. José Capablanca has been called one of the greatest chess players in history. He once was asked how many moves he thought ahead, and his answer was simply, "Just one, the best one."

The same is true in life. Do the homework required to discover your next best move, then make it. Focusing on the vital information will help you make better decisions—it can help get you a contract, land a new client, or build a key relationship sooner. Acting fast doesn't always mean a rapid, knee-jerk response. Acting fast is about knowing how to get to the finish line sooner.

Strategy 5: Persistence pays

Sir James Dyson is the inventor behind the Dyson vacuum cleaner. When asked about his creative new approach to cleaning surfaces, Dyson said, "I made 5,127 prototypes of my vacuum before I got it right. There were 5,126 failures. But I learned from each one. That's how I came up with a solution. So I don't mind failure."

You might be only one failure away from a breakthrough, one rejection away from the opportunity of a lifetime, or one paint stroke away from a masterpiece. Don't give in to fatigue or depression or lack of motivation. Persist, and keep moving forward toward your ideal outcome.

Strategy 6: Press play!

A spirit of imagination and play is essential to success. If you hate what you do, you should envision doing something else. What brings you joy?

You are more likely to take quick action and succeed when you are having fun. Take salespeople, for example. People who love being around people make better sales associates because they are eager to shake someone's hand or to connect with them over the phone. Following your natural inclinations puts a bounce in your step (and money in your wallet).

Personally, I love to paint. Even though painting a portrait on stage only takes me a few minutes, when I'm painting for myself, I can lose myself for hours in the creative process. I often have to pinch myself because I can't believe I make a great living doing what makes me feel most alive.

Now I know most people don't enjoy some elements of their job. Negotiating a merger might be fun, but working with lawyers for weeks or even months on end might bring you down. In situations like this, it's important for you to carve out time in your day to "play." Take 10 minutes during your lunch break to catch up on Facebook or your Twitter or LinkedIn accounts or to send out text or two. During a coffee break, play a quick game of online Scrabble using your smartphone, or go for a short walk outside the building with a coworker. When you add an element of fun to your everyday routine, it will boost your spirits and give you the energy you need to keep moving forward.

Play breaks also are important if you have a large project to finish. After devoting yourself to your work for a reasonable length of time (the actual length will depend on you, the level of project difficulty, and any looming deadlines), reward yourself with a few minutes of fun.

The Pomodoro Technique advocates this time-management method. It was designed by Francesco Cirillo based on the idea that frequent breaks can increase mental agility. After deciding on a task to be completed, set a timer for however long you'd like to work on it before taking a break (typically 25 minutes). When the timer rings, do something else for three to five minutes before resetting the timer and starting work again. After four sets of this (about two hours), take a longer break—say 10 to 15 minutes. Play a couple of rounds of solitaire on your computer, or take a short, brisk walk. It will actually *increase* your overall productivity and make you more effective in your job.

STRATEGY 7: LIGHTEN YOUR LOAD

You can act faster if you are willing to let go of your "stuff." A successful organizational change consultant I worked with for many years was often called in to help executives get unstuck when corporate planning meetings came to a critical impasse. He'd begin by saying, "We're going to do an exercise. Everyone stand up and move three seats to your right."

Invariably someone would ask, "Do we need our stuff?"

America's got Talent

"America's Got Talent Congratulates Robert Channing for a Triumphed Appearence"

America's got Talent

Robert Channing gets a standing ovation during the America's Got Talent show

Simon Cowell gives two thumbs up to Robert Channing

Howard Stern signs painting of himself on stage at the America's Got Talent show

Glue and glitter painting of John Taft the (Chief executive officer) of Royal Bank of Canada's U.S. Wealth Management.

NY Mets Mookie Wilson, Boston Redsox Bill Buckner and the voice of the Syracuse Orange, Matt Park

Invited to do Oprah's Road Show

Gallagher and I right before our performance

John McEntee Jr. with commissioned painting of Donald Trump in the Trump Campaign War Room, Trump Plaza NYC

Eddie Money and I before our show

Michael Cerbelli; The Hot List

Jackie Romano and I at the "Fur Ball"

Robert Channing paints the cast of Fox & Friends. Ainsley Earhardt, Steve Doocy and Pete Hegseth

Robert Channing is blindfolded by Ainsley Earhardt and Steve Doocy and then WOWS them!

bert Channing paints Ainsley rhardt and Steve Doocy.

Robert Channing Paints Donald Trump in GOLD!

Robert Channing goes patriotic.

ROBERT CHANNING

World's Formost Mind Reader & Artist to the Stars

Robert Channing reads serial numbers off of a bill, blind folded for Roger's Conference

Robert with Gene Simmons after the show at the Opryland Hotel Nashville.

Robert and his wife visit with old friends Sheryl & Alice Cooper

Robert Channing paints Donald Trump on Fox & Friends.

Robert paints CEO John Taft of RBC US Wealth Management at the Four Season's Punta Mita Mexico

Performed in England and brought the Royal Family :-)

t Channing paints n Monroe at National ntion in Canada for CIBC

Robert Channing with Dan Patrick of NBC Sports

My manager John McEntee. Remax Corporate Event. Robert paints Steven Tyler before he goes on.

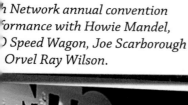

h Network annual convention formance with Howie Mandel, O Speed Wagon, Joe Scarborough Orvel Ray Wilson.

obert Channing mind reading speed painting show in Toronto r Raymond James Financial.

Performed in Monte Carlo and brought the Family :-)

ROBERT CHANNING
Imagination into ART

'Amazing! You couldn't have picked a better subject than me to paint. I Love Your Work!!! I want THIS PAINTING!!! It's going up in my home' -- Howard Stern "King of ALL Media" - *Howard Stern Show*

"NO! STOP! That's INCREDIBLE... That's bananas... I LOVE IT! Robert- Thank you so much!
Serena Williams, Sports Illustrated Sportsperson of the Year for 2015 & World's Women's Tennis Champ

WOW, Robert that was HOT! WOW! I'm The Golden Child!! YOU are an Amazing Painter.
Steve Harvey, Daytime Emmy Award Winner

SPEED
ART
IMAGINATION

SUBCONSCIOUS
MIND READING

NBC

HOWARD STERN
Heidi Klum, Mel B,
Howie Mandel, Nick Cannon &
OVER 14 MILLION TV VIEWERS,
thousands of people and audiences world wide
can't be wrong.

"Robert took his
painting to a whole
NEW LEVEL!
I love it!"
- HOWIE MANDEL
Comedian, Actor

"THE WORLD'S GREATEST MENTALIST.
AMAZING SPEED & GLITTER PAINTER."

ROBERT CHANNING
SUPERNATURAL ENTERTAINER

bert Channing drives a million dollar
blindfolded to promote show at the
nley Theater, Utica, NY

Robert Channing at Radio
City Music Hall, New York City

THE WORLD'S GREATEST MENTALIST

Serena Williams

Women's Professional Tennis Player

Serena Williams and Robert Channing at the CIGNA corporate conference.

Steve Harvey was amazed by Roberts painting of him. Steve Harvey called himself the "Golden Child". :-)

JIM AND JULI BOEHEIM
FOUNDATION

ainting of Jim and
uli Boeheim

Painted Pearl Washington, now hang
at the Carmello K.Anthony Center

Robert paints the super seven of the Final Four
Syracuse Univerity Basketball team.

Painting away!

TODAY

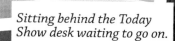

Sitting behind the Today
Show desk waiting to go on.

Dylan Dreyer of the
Today show

signs her
ng the show.

In the Orange Room with
the orange room girls

elle Jones loves her
ng.

Al Roker of the Today
Show.

The consultant would pause dramatically and say, "You know, *that's* the problem. You are all worried about your 'stuff.'" After a moment, he would go on. "Whether it's your department's control or your corner office, you are worried about stuff. It's time to let go and m-o-v-e forward as a team."

Exercise over.

If you want to capitalize on opportunities, and generate momentum in your career, you've got to stop lugging your stuff around. Maybe your stuff is your fixation on getting a promotion, or your concern about not having access to the latest technology to do your work—or a corner office. Such worries sap your energy and divert your focus from what is really important: the task at hand.

You will never get across the finish line first if you keep looking over your shoulder to see where everyone else is or what perks or gadgets they have that you don't. Don't let yourself get distracted by stuff. The lighter your load, the faster you can act with split-second clarity and power.

Strategy 8: Multiply your results

Don't you wish you could clone yourself? You could accomplish so much more, so much faster. While human cloning is not a mainstream option right now, you can still multiply your results in rapid time.

Be creative. Use the latest technology to advance your goals. If you're a business consultant, use your smartphone to take video of your meetings, conferences, and workshops and turn them into downloadable, shareable files to reach a larger audience. If you're a painter, consider making prints of your work and selling them in addition to the originals. If you're a chef, build your personal brand by creating a YouTube channel with short, fun videos that teach people how to cook a variety of dishes in the comfort of their own homes. Technology delivers consumers to your doorstep, and profits to your pocket, with lightning speed.

One of the most lucrative ways to multiply results is by licensing or franchising your business. You'd think that starting a burger franchise would be one of the least-successful ways to make a buck nowadays. In addition to the old standbys McDonald's, Burger King, Wendy's, and all the rest, there are literally thousands of mom-and-pop burger joints scattered across the countryside. However, that didn't stop Danny Meyer from starting up Shake Shack, the burger powerhouse that was established in a kiosk in New York City's Madison Square Park in 2004. The company went public with an IPO just 10 years later—in January 2015—raising $112 million for Shake Shack and valuing the business at a cool $1.6 billion.

You might not be running a burger business, but you can still find ways to multiply the results of your efforts, and you will see your success multiply in record time.

STRATEGY 9: SAY NO WAY MORE OFTEN

I opened this chapter with a story about how saying "yes" opened the door to a string of successes for me. But sometimes saying "no" is an even better answer.

Learning to say no to other people's demands—or to your own tendency to get sidetracked or over-extend yourself—will free you up to focus on key activities that will produce bigger and better results. Since there are only so many hours in a day, the fastest way to get results is to spend most of your time working on things that get you closer to your end zone.

Learn to say no when a colleague asks you to take time out of your already busy day to proofread his report. Learn to say no when the soccer coach asks you to get to the field early to secure a spot for practice. Learn to say no when you start surfing the web for a new gizmo you don't need.

You can still be a team player while saying no, but no one is going to value your time if you don't. Don't allow yourself to be drawn into other people's drama or take on others' problems as your own. You are the star of your own reality show. Set boundaries and keep them. You'll earn their respect, and you'll be ready to act and create rapid results anytime you want.

Fast Action Steps

1. What time do you usually get up in the morning? What would happen if you got up 20 minutes earlier? What could you do with those extra 20 minutes to foster faster results?
2. What activity in your workday do you most fear? Schedule it first thing in the morning.
3. What does your action environment look like? Change one thing in your environment to facilitate increased productivity.
4. What is the main goal you are working toward right now? What can you do to multiply the results of your efforts?
5. Do you have a hard time saying no to people when they ask you to do something? Think about why, and practice saying, "No!"

CHAPTER 6

FAIL FASTER TO SUCCEED SOONER

"Don't you ever let a soul in the world tell you that you can't be exactly who you are."

—LADY GAGA, SINGER, SONGWRITER AND ACTRESS

THIS COULD BE the most important chapter in this book. Why? Because every ounce of you silently screams when you think about failure. If there is even a remote possibility you may fail, your mind starts racing:

I don't want to be embarrassed.
I don't want to let people down.
I don't want to fail!

But here's some good news: You can learn to fail faster so you can succeed sooner. You can reinterpret your failures—even the most painful ones—as valuable lessons and steppingstones on your path to achievement.

Recently, I gave my Imagination into Art presentation at a special event in Mexico. A Fortune 1000 company was rewarding its top sales achievers with food, fun, and wine. I was hired to "edutain" (educate and entertain) more than 250 of the company's best people at a luxury resort. Drinks were flowing, music was playing, and anticipation was building for my performance.

Only the meeting planner and I knew it, but I was about to speed paint a giant glitter portrait of the company's CEO. She told me I needed to be onstage in an hour, which was my cue to get busy. I always like

47

to do a run-through right before each presentation to help me get my mind and body ready to act fast and delight my audience.

But during this particular run-through, I discovered a problem—a really *big* problem.

I use a special glue in my glitter speed-painting demonstrations, and the client had agreed to purchase it for me. But the glue they gave me wasn't right—it wasn't thick and dense, instead, it was thin and watery. When I tested the glue, it ran down my canvas like a popsicle melting in the hot sun.

An overwhelming fear of failure washed over me. I began to sweat and immediately fell into negative thinking: *This could be a giant embarrassment. I might not get paid. This could ruin the company's event—and my reputation.*

I had just 30 minutes before it was time to start. I took a deep breath and made a split-second decision: *I will create my painting come hell or runny glue.* Though I was unable to create a decent painting in my private, pre-show rehearsal, I wasn't going to let that failure stop me from trying to dazzle my audience. After all, the show must go on!

I asked the staff at the resort to put the glue in the freezer for 20 minutes, hoping the cold air would give the glue a thicker consistency. It was just a hunch—that ended up working perfectly. Onstage, I created my three-minute masterpiece without a hitch, and the crowd went crazy. The CEO and his wife loved my massive, glittery portrait of him. Everyone was completely oblivious to the failure I had experienced during my rehearsal—all they saw was an incredible performance. My commitment to success forced me to think and act fast.

If I had not failed during my rehearsal, I would have failed during the live event—in front of 250 people. Failing faster definitely allowed me to succeed sooner.

"There is only one thing that makes a dream impossible to achieve: the fear of failure."

—PAULO COELHO, BRAZILIAN AUTHOR

The following six steps will help you fail—and succeed—more quickly.

The Fail FASTER Formula

As with many things in life, there's a right way and a wrong way to fail. Here's the right way.

Step 1: FRAME failure as a positive result

David Neeleman, the CEO of JetBlue Airways, has a problem shared by many: Attention Deficit Hyperactivity Disorder (ADHD). However, instead of considering this medical condition a deficit in his life, he considers it to be one of his biggest assets. Says Neeleman, "One of the weird things about the type of ADHD I have is, if you have something you are really, really passionate about, then you are really, really good about focusing on that thing." So good, in fact, that he credits his ADHD for the creation of JetBlue's e-ticketing system.

Instead of considering the challenges you face—including failures—to be negatives, frame them as positives, and use them to help you find the success you seek in business, career, and life.

Step 2: ACCELERATE your failure rate

Want to succeed faster? Start failing faster. Once you see that failure is not final but is a path toward your dreams, you will become free to fail faster. Let's be honest: Failure never feels good. But failure should not be taken personally—it's not a reflection of you. Failure is simply part of a learning process. Take the advice of leadership and motivation guru John Maxwell: "Take the 'u' out of failure." If you do, you will find the courage and willingness to try new things and new approaches, which will allow you to fail faster on your road to victory.

Fast failure has become a celebrated philosophy in Silicon Valley, where companies come and go in the wink of an eye. "While the rest of the world recoils at failure," writes Rory Carroll in *The Guardian*, "technology's dynamic innovators enshrine it as a rite of passage en route to success." If you stay positive, don't take failure personally, and fail as fast as you can, you will soon be running circles around your competition.

STEP 3: STUDY THE FAILURES (AND SUCCESSES) OF GREAT ACHIEVERS

You can learn valuable lessons from the men and women who have gone before you. Learn these lessons by:

- Reading biographies and autobiographies about your heroes. You'll be stunned to learn how often these super-achievers experienced failure—and how they were able to bounce back.
- Watching inspiring movies about athletes and teams who discover how to overcome adversity. Three of my personal favorites are: *Rudy, Rocky,* and *Remember the Titans.*
- Watching TED Talks and other inspiring educational programs that will recharge you with courage. One of the best in this area is by Larry Smith, an economics professor at the University of Waterloo, who coaches his students on business startups and career development. He mentored the creators of BlackBerry in their company's infancy. His TED Talk is called, "Why you will fail to have a great career."

STEP 4: TRY AGAIN

It's hard to go back to the plate after striking out—especially in front of a large crowd. Imagine getting back up to bat after striking out 1,383 times. That's what happened to Hank Aaron, the man who in 1974 broke Babe Ruth's record for the most home runs in the history of Major League Baseball—and who held the title until Barry Bonds broke Aaron's record in 2007. The secret to Hank Aaron's success? He swung his bat as many times as it took to connect, because giving up was never an option.

> *"Try again.*
> *Fail again.*
> *Fail better."*

—SAMUEL BECKETT, IRISH PLAYWRIGHT

If you know what you want and are committed to achieving it, don't take no for an answer—even if the no you're hearing is inside your own head. Below is a rejection letter from RSO Records dated May 10, 1979.

Dear Mr. Hewson,

Thank you for submitting your tape of "U2" to RSO. We have listened with careful consideration, but feel it is not suitable for us at present.

We wish you luck with your future career.

Yours sincerely,
Alexander Sinclair
RSO Records (U.K.) Limited

Mr. Hewson is Bono from U2. Aren't you glad he and his band kept playing, despite being rejected by one of the world's top record companies at the time? You should react the same way to your so-called rejections. Dig deep and stay committed to your goal until you achieve it.

STEP 5: ENGAGE YOURSELF IN THE WORK

You are at your core one thing—*energy*—and you have the power to direct your energy in any direction you choose. It's a power that J.K. Rowling—the mega-bestselling author of the *Harry Potter* books series—harnessed to create her own success story.

Today Rowling is a billionaire, but she was not always wealthy. In fact, when she was writing the first of her popular books, she was a single mom on welfare. Like many authors, she experienced massive personal and professional failure, and more rejection letters than I'm sure she'd care to recall. But what sets Rowling apart is a commitment she made to herself to focus her energy on the one thing she felt most equipped to do: write novels. She poured herself into her prose.

"I stopped pretending to myself that I was anything other than what I was, and began to direct all my energy into finishing the only work that mattered to me," she said.

The sooner you try things and fail, the sooner you will discover the best place to focus your energy. When you find that sweet spot where your passion (mind) and talent (body) intersect, success will quickly follow. Later in this book, we will take a closer look at this amazing mind/body connection.

STEP 6: RID YOURSELF OF A WAY OUT

When I was 21, I realized it was time for me to make a serious commitment to my career as a mentalist, and to forget once and for all about a traditional career like being a doctor, lawyer, or used-car salesman. I had spent the entire day calling dozens of college activities directors to try to set up gigs for my mentalist show. All day long I heard the same word: "No." I felt like a failure and I wanted to quit. But in that moment of despair, something happened deep inside of me. I made a split-second decision to stop wasting my time thinking about a career as a doctor, or lawyer, or used car salesman. At that moment, I permanently closed off the path that could carry me back to a safe but unsatisfying life. Knowing there was no turning back, I picked up the phone, and dialed again.

It will work for you too, but you must cut off any and all escape routes and move past failures. Arrange your life and your work so that you have no other choice but to succeed. As champion endurance athlete Travis Macy puts it, "When you have no choice, anything is possible."

FAST ACTION STEPS

Be sure to answer these questions:

1. What would you do if you were certain you could not fail?
2. What has been the biggest failure in your work life? Can you frame it in a new way? In two sentences, describe how it is a blessing in disguise.

3. What can you do to accelerate the rate and number of your failures on the path to your biggest success?

4. Identify a hero from history or from your own life who has worked through his or her failures on the way to important accomplishments.

5. Failure is inevitable, but we often fail doing the wrong things. Name three ways you could fail *on purpose*.

CHAPTER 7

BECOME A MASTER OF MOMENTUM

"Only engage and the mind grows heated.
Begin and then the task will be completed."

~CHARLES MURRAY, MOUNTAIN CLIMBER

IN AN EARLIER chapter I told you about the split-second decision I made to paint a portrait in 90 seconds for *America's Got Talent*. Saying yes to that opportunity—though it stretched me to paint faster than I had ever painted before—created a wonderful wave of momentum in my life. After that experience, I continued to say yes to new opportunities, and my confidence grew exponentially.

I discovered that the old saying is true: Nothing succeeds like success. You'll find that even small wins, when strung together, can create the momentum you need to get "unstuck" and headed in the right direction. If you want to succeed, it's crucial for you to initiate and maximize your momentum.

After painting Howard Stern on *America's Got Talent*, I got some serious traction. Producers invited me to be on *The Steve Harvey Show* and I knocked it out of the park. His audience clapped and cheered as I created a portrait of Steve in mere minutes. I was on a roll.

Still dizzy from that latest response, I soon got a call from the rep of another well-known celebrity. Maybe you've heard of her: Oprah!

The rep told me that Oprah loved my paintings and wanted me to do an event for her. My response was automatic: "Yes!"

But a few minutes after I hung up the phone, I realized I had a problem. Oprah's event dates conflicted with an important family commitment. Being a husband and dad is my highest priority, so I knew I had to put my family first. But before canceling on Oprah, I came up with a split-second solution that kept my momentum going: I offered to paint Oprah from my art studio at home.

It worked! I filmed my creation of Oprah's portrait in my art studio, then sent the film and the painting to Oprah's team. My speed-painting performance was broadcast for Oprah's event, and she was given the enormous painting I had created for her. Everything fell perfectly into place.

Momentum is magical.

Ask yourself, "Where can I win?"

STEPHEN PIERCE, THE SUCCESS SCULPTING COACH

We are all born with specific talents and skills, and it's an unfortunate truth that we can't all be successful at everything. One of the most important steps in your path to success is recognizing *where*—in what medium or field—you have the best chance of accomplishing your goals. This discovery may require a lot of failures in the wrong places, but it will help to remember that Michael Jordan once (not very successfully) tried to play professional baseball.

YOUR MIND AND BODY IN MOTION = MOMENTUM

Long before I was called the world's finest speed painter, I was making my living as a mentalist—someone who can guess the serial number on the $10 bill in your wallet, the date of your wedding anniversary, or what you'll be wearing at my performance—a month from now. My success as a mentalist comes from my understanding that when your mind and your body work together you can do what seems impossible.

Neuroscience has proven this mind-body link time and time again. In an overview on the popular wellness website, WebMD, the phenomenon is explained this way: "Your mind and body are powerful allies. How you think can affect how you feel. And how you feel can affect your thinking."

To experience split-second success, you need to get your brain and your body working together—and quickly. You may not be able to read people's minds, but you can cultivate a synergy between what you think and what you do to get the wheels of your career turning.

It all begins with thoughts. Thoughts are like muscles, and you need to develop your thoughts like you would your biceps. However, thoughts alone aren't enough. You also need to coordinate your mental and physical states. Success lies in activity on the inside *and* outside. Deciding you need to exercise is ineffective for weight loss unless you actually get on a treadmill or swim a few laps.

This combination of mind and body working together can be extremely powerful. People attending Tony Robbins's personal power seminars experience split-second personal transformations. How? By sitting in a chair taking notes? No. They get their brains and bodies up and do his "fire walk." They take off their shoes and walk barefoot on hot coals. And they do it quickly! By keeping their thoughts and feet moving in the same direction they avoid getting burned and they get a taste of what is possible in their lives.

Eight Steps for Becoming a Master of Momentum

> *"The most important thing you can do to achieve your goals is to make sure that as soon as you set them, you immediately begin to create momentum."*
>
> —Tony Robbins

STEP 1: BE CLEAR

Do you know exactly *what* you want? Do you know *where* you are going? If you said yes, good. That's half the battle. But don't confuse random activity with momentum. You won't achieve great things if your focus is diffused. The word is not *more*-mentum. Trying to have it all, or do it all, can lead to burnout and stagnation.

A few pages earlier, I briefly mentioned Michael Jordan's baseball accomplishments. For the most part, no one remembers them. Jordan won three NBA championships with the Chicago Bulls, in 1991, 1992, and 1993. He then took a baseball break in order to try and achieve greatness in a different sport. It didn't work. He struggled with mediocrity. When he returned to basketball he went on to win three more NBA championships—in 1996, 1997, and 1998. You might not be so lucky if you get sidetracked. Don't lose momentum and waste your energy trying to have it all.

One of the best ways to become and remain clear about what you want is to write down your goals. Master success teacher Brian Tracy says, "The speed at which you will begin to achieve your goals after you have written them down is nothing short of miraculous." Putting pen to paper can give you clarity and help you maintain momentum once you find it.

STEP 2: GO!

Don't wait. Get going.

Momentum kicks procrastination in the teeth. Movement is the key to momentum. Ever try moving the steering wheel inside your car while it's parked? It won't budge—at least not more than a wiggle or two. It's much easier to steer a car that is already moving. Do something every day that moves you closer to your goal.

STEP 3: KEEP ROLLING

When someone tells you, "Hey, you're on a roll!" that's a good thing. Once you're in action and moving forward, don't stop. Keep rolling.

Making mistakes is okay, but quitting is not. Do more of what's working, and surround yourself with people who cheer you on.

STEP 4: STAY MOTIVATED

Do you know *why* you want what you want? Think about how reaching your goal will bring you more of what you want. Think about how you will experience more meaning, more money, more energy, more opportunities, and more freedom. This internal motivation is like rocket fuel for the soul.

STEP 5: GET UP WHEN YOU FALL DOWN

You will hit speed bumps along the way to the success you seek, but don't back off. Making mistakes is part of the learning curve of success. Learn from those mistakes and keep moving forward. You need persistence and tenacity to succeed, and an ability to lick your wounds and move on.

STEP 6: ACCELERATE YOUR EFFORTS

Remember why you are in the race: to win. Focus on the finish line and don't slow down as you near it. Dig deep and finish strong. You'll experience an enormous energy boost—like a second wind, or a runner's high—when you accelerate toward your big finish.

STEP 7: GET OVER IT

I'm talking about the finish line. Get over it. Get through it. Get across it. If you were clear about what said you wanted in Step 1, you'd know exactly what getting over the finish line looks like. When you cross it, hold up your trophy and celebrate. Then quickly proceed to Step 8.

STEP 8: DON'T STOP

Once you have momentum, don't lose it. Once you cross your finish line, set another goal. Keep moving forward. It is much easier to maintain motion than it is to restart it after inertia has set in. Stephen Covey suggests in his book *The 7 Habits of Highly Effective People* that you need to take time to sharpen the saw. This means you have to set aside time for resting and recharging your batteries. But you can't lounge around so long that your saw starts to rust. Get in the habit of keeping your mind and your body in motion and looking past your recent finish line to a new horizon.

Go for the Gold

The famous saying is, "*Go* for the gold," not "*Wait* for the gold." If you want to succeed, you've got to start moving. Get some momentum going. Who knows what you'll discover when you start putting one foot in front of the other? Like a couple in Northern California discovered, treasure may await you when you get off your sofa.

A couple years ago, the couple—who anonymously went by John and Mary in news reports—were walking their dog on their property. Mary spotted a rusty old can, and though she saw through the cracks that there was something inside, the couple kept walking. Ten paces later, the pair found another can. Then another. John grabbed his metal detector and their search unearthed eight tin cans filled with 1,400 gold coins. Experts estimate that it was a $10 million discovery! Some of the coins sold for $17,500 each.

Now I want you to notice two things about this story. The first: John and Mary found the gold treasure in their own backyard. Second: They found it while they were outside—moving, walking, digging, and discovering.

It's another — albeit serendipitous — example that the success you seek may be right under your nose. Perhaps the only thing standing between you and your treasure is the courage to take that first step, and the discipline to create and maintain your momentum.

Fast Action Steps

1. Take a moment to write down a clear objective you want to achieve.
2. What can you do today to move toward that goal?
3. Which distractions can you eliminate that will get you going and keep you rolling? Examples: log out of Facebook, or find peaceful surroundings where you can work uninterrupted.
4. What would feel like a small win to you right now? How can you build on it?

CHAPTER 8

SPLIT-SECOND LEADERSHIP

"If you want to go fast, go alone.
If you want to go far, go with others."

AFRICAN PROVERB

A FEW YEARS ago I became super busy—too busy, really—giving performances across North America and around the world. It was exciting, but as I mentioned, my biggest priority is my family, not my fame, and I was starting to feel out of balance. I had a big dilemma: I wanted to continue to grow my income, but I also wanted to stop going out on the road so much so I could spend more time with my wife and young kids.

People tell me that I do amazing things, but there's only one of me to go around. And there is only one you. So how can we expand our influence and income without working ourselves to death?

GET SMART

The solution to this dilemma, I decided, was to invest in myself. My goal was to learn more about business and leadership so that I could work smarter instead of harder. I invested many thousands of dollars in training, courses, consultations, and seminars to promote my development as a business leader. You don't have to spend that much, but you do have to invest in yourself. To start, build yourself a library of books and courses on leadership and success, and watch online videos about successful people you admire and want to emulate.

One of the themes that emerged for me during my studies was the importance of finding a mentor. By tapping into a mentor's lifetime experience, and learning in a conversation what it took them decades to perfect, you can often get a fast pass to success.

MENTORS HELP INCREASE YOUR SPEED OF SUCCESS

One of the courses I took during my studies was called, "How to Book Yourself as a Performer or Speaker." This was a self-study course developed by a successful entertainer, entrepreneur, and friend of mine. I wanted to take my training to the next level, so I hired him as a consultant and flew out to California to work with him. The one-day meeting we had was another turning point for me. In that one day, I reaped the benefits of more than a quarter century of this mentor's hard work and well-honed success models.

The first thing he said hooked me: "Robert, you can generate revenue while you play with your kids at home." That is exactly what I wanted to do. In the next several hours he outlined how I could start booking other entertainers and speakers in addition to booking my own events. It was like a lightning bolt hit me: *I can serve my clients by providing them with other powerful, amazing presenters like me, while spending more time with my family.* I am also an in-demand mentor and resource to many speakers, business leaders, and performers, and I help them create their own split-second success.

> *"Teams make you better than you are, multiply your value, enable you to do what you do best, allow you to help others do their best, give you more time, provide you with companionship, help you fulfill the desires of your heart, and compound your vision and effort."*

—JOHN MAXWELL, LEADERSHIP EXPERT

After my meeting with one of my mentors and coaches, I didn't hesitate to start a new speakers bureau—PowerPerformers.com. We provide meeting and event planners with high-impact speakers, celebrities, and entertainers. This business has generated many millions of dollars for the presenters we manage, but more important, lives have been touched and meetings transformed into unforgettable memories.

And for me? It has brought more income and more time for me to cheer at my daughter's crew meets and my sons' baseball and basketball games. Launching our new business hasn't been easy, but on so many different levels it's been well worth it.

If you want to get to the next level in your work life, even if you work for someone else, you must become a leader. If you are not a natural-born leader and you need a little help, find a mentor who can draw out the leader in you. It might also help to follow the 10 Leadership Secrets I have learned from growing my business into an international operation that serves more than 2,000 colleges, corporations, and associations around the world.

THE 10 MASTER KEYS TO LEADERSHIP SUCCESS

MASTER KEY 1: SHARE YOUR VISION

One thing has struck me about the reactions I get from my speed-painting work: People get emotionally involved with the picture I'm creating. Whether it's a famous celebrity, a familiar landmark like the Statue of Liberty, or even a billionaire CEO, the response is the same. They are all captivated when I paint a picture for them. They are especially transfixed when I paint a picture *about* them.

This is what leaders do: *We draw people into our stories by painting them into the picture.* You are probably not a speed painter, but you can harness this power simply by telling your story, and by sharing your vision.

This is *not* the same as sharing information with others. Managers have charts, graphs, and use PowerPoint presentations. Leaders tell stories—and they inspire as a result.

What is your story, and how does it move people toward a compelling vision for their future? It doesn't matter what type of business you're in, as a leader you are in the *inspiration* business. Robert Pollard, a prolific indie rock songwriter, captures this truth in his song *Run Wild*: "Every heart needs inspiration."

Master Key 2: Build your team

People are silently begging you to lead them. You must ensure that each of your team members knows:

- Where you are going
- Who's riding on the airplane with you
- That the right people are in the right seats

You may have noticed that I used the example of an airplane instead of the more common bus metaphor. I want you to succeed faster than a bus can travel. Think of yourself as the pilot of your organization. In the United States, airline pilots have a better than 99.9 percent success rate—that is, they almost always get to their destination instead of crashing and burning. Why? They know where they are going, and they have the support of a great crew. A pilot's success depends not only on his or her own skills and experience, but also on the co-pilots, safety crews, and air-traffic controllers with whom they work. Professional pilots also are really good at the two most important parts of a flight: taking off and landing.

You must master these two areas with your organization, too, but you can't do it all by yourself. To succeed, you need to surround yourself with a great team.

Master Key 3: Be transparent

I told you earlier about how I painted a giant portrait of Howard Stern on *America's Got Talent* and the amazed reaction on the judges' faces. Now let me tell you the secret to Stern's success. It's not his radio show. It's not his raunchy humor.

The secret to Stern's success is his transparency. He consistently tells it like it is—both about himself, and about those around him. Stern once said that to get to the next level, you have to learn to open up a whole lot more than you naturally might be inclined to. If you have a track record of being transparent, those around you will believe what you say without hesitation. It has often been said that "he who hesitates is lost." If you want to win and win quickly, cultivate transparency.

Master Key 4: Create transformation

Back to our plane metaphor: Danny Cox was a supersonic jet test pilot. He became a master of speed and went on to write one of the best books ever written about being a leader. In *Leadership When the Heat Is On*, Cox emphasizes that, just as he learned how to break through the sound barrier in supersonic flight, a leader must help others break through their own barriers.

Leaders make new realities for themselves and for others. Everyone wants to grow, discover, and learn. Your job is not to make life *easy* for the people you lead, but to help make it *meaningful*. You do that by inviting, encouraging, and facilitating change. If the members of your team are excited about the transformations taking place in their lives, they will invest more of themselves in the process, and the entire team will benefit. Personal transformation is like weight on the throttle: It makes things go faster. If every member of your team is undergoing a transformation, the speed and scope of your project will increase exponentially.

Master Key 5: Design your template

It's tempting to build your organization around the personalities of your people. "Hey, Mary is good with money, let's have her do accounting." "John is very likable. Let's put him in charge of sales."

Don't do that. Run your business or organization based on a template of processes. Implement a system of production that will make each department run smoothly, regardless of who is carrying out the operations. This is the competitive edge behind Starbucks, Amazon, Apple, and other great companies. Yes, they hire great people. But they also plug them into a winning template.

Don't make the success of your operation dependent on any one personality—even your own. Document everything you do and continually improve the systems that create your success.

MASTER KEY 6: HANDLE TROUBLE

Have you ever broken down the word "responsibility?" It may be the word that best captures the essence of leadership. If you look closely, you'll realize it's actually two words in one: *response* + *ability*. When problems arise—as they always do—a true leader is able to not only respond, but also respond quickly.

Just weeks after Mary Barra arrived at General Motors in 2014 to lead the company as CEO, she initiated the recall of what eventually amounted to 2.6 million vehicles with faulty ignition switches linked to fatal accidents. While GM's (and Barra's) response to the PR crisis that followed the announcement was considered to be "unimpressive" by some in the media, Mary Barra quickly realized the severity of the problem, and she handled it. Says David Johnson of PR firm Strategic Vision, "She called reporters to General Motors' headquarters and addressed the issue. She pledged to fix faulty ignition switches…She also apologized."

Bucking a dysfunctional corporate culture, Barra told her employees at a town hall meeting, "I never want to put this behind us. I want to put this painful experience in our collective memories."

If you are not solving problems, you are not a leader. If you want to enjoy split-second success, like Barra, you must be ready to make difficult decisions fast.

MASTER KEY 7: SET A TIME FRAME

When I first started appearing on national TV shows with my speed painting, what seemed to blow people away the most was not just what I was painting, but that I was painting full masterpieces in minutes. This helped me realize that great leaders make great use of time.

Steve Jobs was famous for the outrageous demands he placed on his employees—including developing great products and delivering on seemingly impossible deadlines. Today, this tradition of excellence is upheld by Apple vice president Kim Vorrath, who is in charge of project management for the company's iOS and OS X operating system software, a critical position for Apple, which relies on smooth rollouts of its latest-and-greatest products.

When the iPhone was originally being prepared for release in 2007, Apple employees were expected to devote themselves fully to the effort to ensure the new product introduction took place on time. Anything less than 100 percent devotion to the task at hand was unacceptable. As reported by Jessica Lessin, then a Wall Street Journal technology writer,

> *During a tense time before the first release of iOS software in 2007, Ms. Vorrath grew irate when a colleague was heading home early before another marathon weekend meeting. She slammed her office door so hard that the doorknob broke, and she locked herself in. Mr. Forstall grabbed a baseball bat to try to break her out, people who worked at Apple at the time recall.*

While great leaders don't necessarily need to slam doors to make their point, they do paint a vision for their people that is inspiring. Leaders not only paint pictures for people, they see to it that those pictures are created in seconds, minutes, years, or decades, through setting deadlines and providing the resources needed to meet them. For great leaders, time is of the essence.

MASTER KEY 8: MASTER TECHNOLOGIES

As a master of speed, you must ensure that your team is using the best technologies for your industry. According to the MIT Sloan School of Management, companies that promote innovative technology are at least 25 percent more profitable than those that don't. You may think you can't afford new technology, but the truth is you can't afford *not* to have it.

This doesn't mean you need every new gadget that comes along. Support your team with the tools that will deliver exceptional service to each and every customer with laser-like precision.

As a leader, you don't necessarily need to know how the technology works behind the scenes. But you do have to acknowledge and embrace the reality of living in a world where rapidly changing technology can lead to innovation overnight. There are newer and better ways of doing *your* business. Explore them. Harness them. Create a corporate culture that fosters the mindset that speed and technology are good.

MASTER KEY 9: BUILD TRUST

One of the most important business thinkers of our time is Simon Sinek. Read everything he has written and watch every clip of him that you can, including his TED talk about leadership called, "Why good leaders make you feel safe." Your job as a leader is to help your team—and your customers—know that they can trust you.

A key ingredient to gaining someone's trust is to always keep your word. If you can't keep a promise that you made, immediately let people know there is a problem and work out a mutually agreeable solution. As a leader, trust is your most valuable currency. Guard it. Nurture it. Help it grow.

Trust is important because our brains are wired to make instant judgments. Can I eat this food? Is this a safe place to walk? Will this person put me at risk? Most of the time we are not conscious of our brain's judgmental activity—it happens automatically without our awareness. But you and I are wired to test everything and everyone who comes our way based on one question: *Do I feel that I can trust him or her?* If you pass the test, positive and productive relationships can develop.

Levels of trust are important in relationships too. The more trustworthy you are, the easier and faster it will be for you to influence change with the help of others. You will be able to create higher levels of productivity and team cohesiveness.

One of the best ways to get people to trust *you*, is to trust *them*. Give others the respect you think you deserve. Become more trusting and you will begin to build your own trustworthiness almost immediately.

MASTER KEY 10: TRANSFER YOUR AUTHORITY

Fast-acting leaders become great leaders because they delegate. This means much more than giving other people to-do lists. Leadership is about empowering your team members by *sharing your authority with them.*

Are you communicating to your people that they have the freedom to think and act immediately, without getting your approval on every little thing? If not, you're telling them that all progress depends on you. This kills the spirit of an organization, and it slows it down. Even LeBron James, the best basketball player in the NBA, can't win a championship by himself.

Let your people know that:

- You believe in them.
- You will back them up.
- You want them to succeed and will share the credit with them.

FAST ACTION STEPS

Take these questions and discuss them with your team. The answers you hear will enlighten you and spur your group to higher and faster success.

1. How is the level of *trust* in our organization? What can we do to repair and improve it?
2. Do we have a clear sense of where we are going? Do we know how we will get there?
3. Do we have the right systems in place for running our company?
4. Do we have the right people performing those functions?
5. Do we have a clear sense of our purpose and a time frame for completing our biggest goals?

CHAPTER 9

SPLIT-SECOND CREATIVITY

*"We consider the artist a special sort of person.
It is more likely that each of us is a special sort of artist."*

—ELSA GIDLOW, POET AND PHILOSOPHER

I HAVE SPENT nearly 30 years in the world of entertainment and the arts. And after almost every speed-painting performance, I hear the same thing: "I could never do that in a million years. You are so lucky that you were born with that special gift." Or, "I wish I could create something beautiful like that—and so fast! But I'm not an artist." Or, "Incredible! You must have gone to art school for years to learn that!"

While these comments are flattering, they are based on a false assumption—that creativity is reserved for just a select few.

The truth is that *everyone* possesses the creative energy they need to produce something beautiful. Maybe you're not a painter, but creativity is not the birthright of artists alone. This chapter is designed to help you discover your creative core.

There are many myths regarding creativity. I love myths, but the ones I've listed below are deadly to your personal creativity.

- You are either born creative or you're not.
- Artists are emotional, unpredictable, and flaky.
- Creativity is a lonely path.
- You create best from an "Aha!" flash of inspiration.

- The starving artist stereotype is true.
- You can't have a real job and be an artist.

People believe these myths because they haven't bothered to question them. Everyone used to believe that the Earth was flat, but just because an idea is repeated over and over doesn't make it true. I'm going to dispel some of these myths and prove that you *do* have the seeds of creativity within you. Follow the secrets to split-second creativity below and your creative self will bloom.

> *"Magic is easy ... once you know the secret."*

> —MARSHALL BRODEIN, WIZZO THE WIZARD

8 SECRETS TO SPLIT-SECOND CREATIVITY

1. YOU ARE AN ARTIST.

There is nothing mystical or magical about artists. They are simply individuals who respond to stimuli in their environment in creative ways, using various media to express how they feel and what they see. Painters use brushes, musicians use instruments, and writers use words.

Entrepreneurs, company executives, and sales reps are artists too.

Think about it: Each of the businesspeople listed above makes something from nothing, just like artists do. Entrepreneurs take a vision and turn it into a viable business. Company executives facilitate the development of new products, or oversee the merger of two companies to create something completely new. Sales reps use phone calls, print materials, and handshakes to bring new clients to the table. They all produce something from nothing, using environmental cues to inspire and drive them.

No matter who you are or what you do, you are an artist. Embrace the creative side of your nature, and give substance to your dreams. The canvas of your life is waiting—create a masterpiece. The sooner you give in to your creativity, the sooner the world can see your brilliance.

2. CREATIVE PEOPLE ARE ORGANIZED.
You've probably heard it said that artists thrive on chaos. Not so. We (and I'm including you here) thrive on order.

Here is the checklist I use before I hit the stage and create a masterpiece in minutes.

- WHO am I painting today?
- What FEELING do I want to capture here?
- Is my CANVAS ready?
- Do I have the proper LIGHTING?
- Are the MICROPHONE and MUSIC cued up?
- Am I all set with BRUSHES and PAINT?
- Are the GLUE and GLITTER ready for the big reveal?
- Does the emcee have my pre-scripted INTRODUCTION?
- Is my WATER BOTTLE pre-set onstage?

What does your creativity checklist look like? Set yourself up for more-creative wins (and faster results) by getting organized before you launch your projects.

3. ARTISTS THRIVE WITHIN LIMITS.
Steve Penley, Coca-Cola's unofficial artist-in-residence, discovered his greatness when he *had* to paint. A friend needed 15 to 20 paintings to cover the bare walls of his restaurant, and he asked Penley, an art school graduate, to help out. That in itself is a big undertaking for one artist, and Penley was given only four days to complete the paintings. Not one to shy away from a challenge, Penley rolled up his sleeves and started to work.

When he began the project, he had only a vague idea of his own personal style. He discovered the bright-and-bold strokes that would later make him famous by painting furiously in the confines of a serious deadline.

Penley's ability to not only paint well, but to paint within the limits of a contract, caught the attention of a number of the nation's top companies. He continued to produce exceptional paintings on the timelines dictated by the corporate world. Word spread, and Coke eventually hired him full time. Penley landed this rare opportunity due in large part to his ability to thrive within limits.

What is limiting you? Time? Money? Supplies? Use those limits to activate or accelerate your creativity. Working within limits may initiate the creative breakthrough you've been searching for.

4. CREATIVITY LOVES COMPANY.

"Me. We."

—MUHAMMAD ALI

Muhammad Ali is arguably the most famous and most creative athlete of the twentieth century. He was a boxer, dancer, magician, poet, clown, and spokesman. He called himself "The Greatest," and who could disagree? He backed up his words with wins.

When asked to write a poem about his philosophy of success, Ali submitted the simple words: "Me. We."

Ali was the greatest, but he knew that creativity was about collaboration, not being a lone wolf. Ali created his magic with opponents, reporters, promoters, managers, trainers, his family, fans, and even TV personalities such as sports journalist Howard Cosell.

Creative people have minds of their own, but they are never alone. If you want to connect with creativity faster, think: *Who is cheering me on? With whom am I collaborating? Who else has a stake in this project? Where do I need help and who can provide it?*

5. STOP TRYING TO BE AN ORIGINAL

The "Fab Four"—the Beatles—gained a reputation for being creative geniuses and artistic originals. Years after they broke up, Paul McCartney alone has earned the title "most successful composer in history" for the many songs he wrote—with the Beatles, with his group Wings, and during the course of his long solo career.

I *love* the Beatles.

But I want to tell you something: The Beatles did not invent rock or pop music. They borrowed heavily from Buddy Holly, Chuck Berry, Little Richard, Elvis, and even Bob Dylan. They created their most famous album, *Sgt. Pepper's Lonely Hearts Club Band*, after hearing the latest record by the Beach Boys—*Pet Sounds*—and wanting to do it their way.

Stop trying to be an original; just be the best you. No one can compete with that.

6. CRITICISM IS YOUR FRIEND

One of the biggest deterrents to people tapping into their creativity is their fear of criticism or rejection. This fear can be intense because the product of your creativity is a piece of your soul out there in the world for everyone to see. That's what makes criticism hurt. But if you learn to not take criticism personally, you can use critical comments to help you hone your skills, modify your product, or recalibrate your direction. You will amplify and accelerate your success when you take constructive criticism to heart.

7. MAKING MONEY IS AN ART FORM

In her outstanding book, *Make Art, Make Money: Lessons from Jim Henson*, Elizabeth Hyde Stevens disproves the notion that you can't be an artist *and* a successful businessperson.

Jim Henson was the brilliant creative force behind *Sesame Street* and *The Muppets*. He also was a charismatic entrepreneur who leveraged his creativity into what are now widely recognized brands. These brands have enjoyed immense financial and fan-based success in the film, television, toy, and literary industries. Henson turned his imagination into puppets with personalities, and then turned his business acumen into a puppet empire.

8. Progress beats perfection.

When it comes to art, there is no such thing as perfection. Beauty, after all, is in the eye of the beholder. Artists must acknowledge this truth or they will never complete their pieces. Could Michelangelo have spent a few more years working on the Sistine Chapel? Of course. Would it have been more beautiful? Would we have loved it more? Perhaps, but the grand work he crafted on that ceiling is amazing as it is, and after five years it was time for him to move on.

Creativity is a process that needs progress. It also needs a finish line. How many rewrites do you need to finish that report? How many design changes are required before you know your new product line is ready for release? At some point, you've got to know when you're done and let it go.

Once you turn off the inner voice that demands perfection, you will be free to create without editing yourself along the way. Only then can you experience the joy that comes from split-second creativity.

Fast Action Steps

1. Do you see yourself as a creative person? If not, why not?
2. Have you ever experienced financial benefits from your creative endeavors? What did you create?
3. Do you edit yourself as you create? Concentrate on quieting the editor in your brain as you work through your next project.
4. Does criticism from others deflate or motivate you? The next time someone criticizes your input, work, or level of participation,

step back and see whether you can use anything in his or her comments to improve your creative process.

5. What limits do you feel are hindering your creative work? Can you reframe the limitations so they work in your favor?

CHAPTER 10

Split-Second Change

"To change one's life:
1. Start immediately.
2. Do it flamboyantly.
3. No exceptions."

—William James, father of American psychology

If you visit GoodReads.com—a wonderful source for provocative quotations on almost any topic—the number of inspiring statements about change will astonish you. There are more than 3,000 of them. Ranked by readers, the most popular quote is from Mahatma Gandhi: "Be the change that you wish to see in the world." Make a mental note: Be the change.

The second most popular quote is from an ad campaign for Apple Computer:

Here's to the crazy ones. The misfits. The rebels. The troublemakers. The round pegs in the square holes. The ones who see things differently. They're not fond of rules. And they have no respect for the status quo. You can quote them, disagree with them, glorify, or vilify them. About the only thing you can't do is ignore them. Because they change things. They push the human race forward. And while some may see them as the crazy ones, we see genius. Because the people who are crazy enough to think they can change the world, are the ones who do.

In both quotations, you'll notice that neither suggests waiting for change. Instead, they suggest that it's up to us to create it. In just two decades, Gandhi led a non-violent revolution that freed India from 200 years of British rule. And in two decades, Steve Jobs and Apple transformed our world with personal computers, tablets, iPhones, animated films, and digital publishing.

ARE YOU READY TO MAKE CHANGE?

Conversations about change usually revolve around the rapid changes we see in climate, technology, science, politics, and the economy. The emphasis is almost always on how we need to *adapt* to change. But adapting to change is not the focus of this chapter or this book.

Split-second change is *proactive*. It is rapid transformation you can *make* for yourself and your organization. The following "10 Techniques for Making Change Happen Fast" will help you make changes more quickly than you ever thought possible. If you apply what you learn, you'll be a quick-change artist in no time.

10 STEPS FOR MAKING CHANGE HAPPEN FAST

STEP 1: MAKE A DECISION

Decisions are the catalysts of change. Nothing happens until *you decide* to make it happen. One clear decision has the power to change the trajectory of your life forever. If you don't believe me, just ask Jimmy Fallon.

I met Fallon for the first time during the summer of 1995. I was driving to my performance at the College of Saint Rose in Albany, N.Y., when I got a call from Rita McLaughlin, the student association advisor at the college. Rita asked if I could give some show business advice to a student who worked in her office. He wanted to be a professional comedian.

"No problem," I said. "Have him meet me after the show."

Later that night, Rita introduced me to Fallon. He was nervous and wiry. He said he was performing at local comedy clubs and was thinking about going after his big break. But he was concerned that his parents would be upset if he dropped out of college. I reminded him that the college wasn't going anywhere. He could always go back if his comedy career didn't work out.

"They're holding auditions for *Saturday Night Live*," he said with excitement. "Should I just go for it?"

"Yes," I said immediately, "Go for it!" It's the same thing I would say to anyone asking that question. I remember that Fallon's eyes lit up. His decision to *go for it* ultimately led him to *The Tonight Show Starring Jimmy Fallon*.

Every breakthrough achievement starts with a split-second decision. What decision could you make today?

Step 2: Make priorities

Setting priorities can be challenging, but you must begin by deciding what is most important to you. The sooner you figure out your priorities, the sooner you will see positive change in all areas of your life.

I've told you that my family is my first priority, and all of my business decisions—from the distances I travel to performances, to how I run my Power Performers speakers bureau—flow from that initial priority. I didn't experience rapid advancement in my career until I learned to align my business plans with my desire to put my family first.

You can experience split-second change simply by figuring out what your top priorities are, and then changing your schedule to focus on them. Scott Grossberg, author of *The Most Magical Secret: 4 Weeks to an Ecstatic Life*, says it this way: "I manifest my intentions through my calendar." Having a clear list of priorities helps you work smarter, not harder.

Step 3: Make it stop

Stop wasting time. It's slowing you down and handcuffing your ability to execute the change you need to succeed. Do you need to stop getting caught up in office gossip? Do you need to stop surfing the web every time you turn on your computer?

Whatever it is you need to stop, stop it—cold turkey. If it's not serving you, if it's not getting you closer to your goals, let it go...now. The sooner you stop wasting your time, the sooner you will experience empowering change.

Step 4: Make it work

Things will not always go according to plan. You need to face every challenge head on if you are going to experience the change you seek. Be persistent, be flexible, be professional, and you will be successful.

Not long ago my road to success was challenged by a drunk CEO. I was performing for a prestigious client I had landed after my appearance on *America's Got Talent*. The audience was filled with well-connected event planners looking for talent for the many major companies they represented. This one show could take my career to the next level. I had to "kill it," as we say in show biz.

My big moment began after the CEO introduced me. He handed me the mic, but as I started talking he grabbed it back and spent the next 10 minutes slurring an apology to a client he forgot to mention during the awards ceremony. He eventually gave me back the mic and meandered offstage.

All smiles, I turned to the audience and got on with my show. About 20 minutes later, right when I was about to surprise and amaze them, the CEO stumbled back onstage, grabbed the mic again, rambled on about something, and stumbled off the stage once more. He interrupted my show a total of three or four more times, but each time I stayed composed and deflected his interruption into a funny part of my performance. In the end, I got a standing ovation, a huge check, and several offers to perform at other events. And if truth be told, I loved it. Why? Because it was a challenge. I faced it, made it work, and was richly rewarded for my efforts.

No matter what you are working on or toward, challenges will come. Find a way to make things work using your experience and the tools you have at hand. You, too, will be richly rewarded.

Step 5: Make believe

Want to see magical results happen in your life—fast? Then make believe you already are who you want to become, and act like you have already arrived. This is known in the world of personal growth development as the "Act As If" principle.

Way before Steven Spielberg became a successful Hollywood producer and director, he snuck onto the Universal movie lot and began to explore. The workers were so impressed by his enthusiasm that they gave him a pass to come back and watch the directors at work. He did—again and again—eventually earning an unpaid internship in the editorial department. Networking with everyone he met, he would become the youngest television producer in Universal history. Eventually, he made the right connections—and had the talent to back up his bravado—and became the internationally acclaimed moviemaker he always knew he was.

Acting as though you already are who you desire to be will help you make the changes you need to make to get you there faster. For example:

- *How would a healthy person eat?* Eat like that.
- *What would a successful real estate broker do to increase her business?* Do that.
- *How would Will Smith or Jennifer Lawrence approach this audition?* Prepare like that.

Step 6: Make a covenant

Early in my career, I made a solemn commitment to honor the performers' motto, "The show must go on." This commitment immediately separated me from the hundreds of flaky entertainers who clog the marketplace. To me, contracts are sacred covenants. My clients can rest assured that if I tell them I will be at their event, I'll be there. I won't even let health issues stand in the way of keeping my word.

I once had two seizures while flying home from Arizona. When the plane landed, I was rushed to a hospital and pumped full of medicine. My regular physician was eventually able to examine me, and he diagnosed my episodes on the airplane not as seizures, but as vasovagal responses—a condition where your heart and body begin to shut down due to stress, fatigue, or lack of sleep.

My doctor advised me to take a few months off, but that next week I had two events scheduled. Knowing that keeping my commitment to my clients was critically important to my reputation of being trustworthy, I decided not to cancel my performance. Instead, I took two days off and hired a driver so I could relax and recharge while on the road.

My solution worked. I stayed healthy, and both events went off without a hitch. If I weren't so committed to honoring my contracts, it would have been easy to back out of my engagements. Thankfully, my covenant kept me on track.

Having a reputation for being reliable has helped me book more than 3,000 events in the last 20 years. Have you made a covenant to yourself or to others to show up and be great?

STEP 7: MAKE A MOVE

Changing your work, home, or social environment can result in amazing progress toward your goals. Even small changes in your surroundings will catapult you across the finish line.

Ace rock guitarist Eric Clapton was rumored to have locked himself in his room for a year to hone his prodigious playing skills. It turned out to be an exaggeration, but Clapton did break away from his regular routine and stayed with a friend—Ben Palmer—for a month while he practiced the techniques that would ultimately reveal his signature style.

Where can you go to get going? Will surrounding yourself with creative people help draw out your own creativity? Or do you need to find solitude to spark success? Discover what works best for you, and do everything in your power to move to where you can make change quickly.

Step 8: Make it pay

If money matters to you, it can be the perfect motivation you need to make change quickly. You live in a world narrated by your own self-talk, so figure out a way to value yourself, and others will value you, too.

When I first began to make big money for my keynote presentations, I had to fight feelings of unworthiness. I didn't think I should receive so much money when I was having so much fun doing what I do. Fortunately I now see that even though I'm having fun I'm also providing my clients with a unique, mind-blowing product that is wowing their colleagues and making everyone look good.

Are you helping people save time? Get better results? Improve their relationships? Enhance their health? Then you deserve to get paid for it. And the more value you provide to others, the more financial reimbursement you should expect to receive in the form of a raise, increased sales, or the ability to charge higher prices or rates.

Step 9: Make it up as you go

Masters of improvisational comedy such as Tina Fey create new characters and hilarious skits on the spot. They say *yes* to whatever is happening in the moment, and react immediately—without second-guessing themselves or the situation. These same elements—speed and fluidity—are key elements to successful change in your business and personal endeavors, too.

Just like an improv comedian, you need to practice "making it up as you go." Trust your instincts and your ability to react.

Step 10: Make it so

Patrick Stewart created a memorable character as Captain Jean-Luc Picard in *Star Trek: The Next Generation*. Remember his straightforward command? "Make it so," he said.

Have you met people who just flat-out get things done—people who do what they say they are going to do? Become one of those people. Successful people don't wait—they create. As the captain of your life, you also need to give yourself that command: Make it so. It will only take only a split second to transform your life into a masterpiece.

Fast Action Steps

- Can you come up with 15 actions you can take to move more quickly toward your biggest goal? Write them down *now.*
- Cut that list down to the top three actions you should take right away.
- Which one of those three action items will help you make the biggest change you need to make to reach your goal?
- Will you do it? When? Put it on your calendar.
- Of the 10 change-makers you just read about, which one will you incorporate into your life right away?

AFTERWORD

"The way to predict your future is by creating it today!"

—ROBERT CHANNING

HERE'S A QUOTE I really like, often attributed to Albert Einstein: "Everybody is a genius. But if you judge a fish by its ability to climb a tree, it will live its whole life believing that it is stupid."

Each one of us is unique—there's no one else in the world just like us—and we all excel in some special way. Whether it's being an amazing financial planner, a terrific teacher, a great parent, or the best salesperson in your organization—every one of us has genius within us.

So I ask you, what is *your* genius?

I am blessed beyond all words to be able to make a career doing what I love most: helping others find their own genius and tap into their full potential. While some may see my speed painting, mind reading, and other performances as just a lot of razzle-dazzle, there's much more to it than that. When I perform in front of a corporate team, or give a keynote for an association, or go on stage for a conference with thousands in attendance, I'm showing that the impossible is indeed possible. I'm demonstrating that each and every one of us can perform remarkable—even amazing—feats. By unlocking the power of our minds, we can achieve extraordinary results.

Each of us has this power within us. We can turn it on—and reap the benefits—anytime we want to.

"To sit back and let fate play its hand out and never in-fluence it is not the way man was meant to operate."

—John Glenn, Astronaut and U.S. Senator

I sincerely hope you will have the opportunity to experience one of my speed painting or mind reading performances at your own event. I want you to feel the excitement and positive energy that comes over the room the split second each person begins to explore his or her own potential. I'm not exaggerating when I say this single event has the power to lift your organization to an entirely new level of success.

When preparation meets opportunity, you will experience your own "Split-Second Success." I've worked on my craft for almost three decades, and without hesitation I can tell you – the most extraordinary, and often unexpected, achievements have come as a direct result of my ability to make split-second decisions.

It's worked for me, and it will work for you!

Robert Channing

Performance Speed Painter, Glitter Painter and Extreme Action Artist with a Mental Twist...

You've heard of fast food. But what about fast art? Extreme action artist and world-famous mentalist Robert Channing will whip up masterpieces in minutes and create portraits right before your eyes on a 5 by 6-foot canvas in 4 to 7 minutes. These paintings in some instances are merely passing thoughts from members of the audience. Channing reads their minds then paints their thoughts on canvas. It's truly amazing to see...

Channing's one-of-a-kind portraits of Einstein, Marilyn Monroe, Jimi Hendrix, Martin Luther King, Jr., and the Statue of Liberty are among the 70 iconic figures from the world of music, movies, sports, art, and history he has created using his fingertips, palms, elbows and up to four paint brushes in each hand. For inspiration, and to rev up his audience, he choreographs his movements to powerful music that stimulates the senses. No wonder people go nuts over Robert's glitter paintings. His performance is a showstopper and the paintings are amazing to see in person!

Mind reader

"Imagine A Sure-Fire Way to Captivate, Entertain, and Motivate Your Attendees at Your Next Meeting or Event ..."

"A Meeting Planner's Dream"

Is your audience tough to please? Are your speakers putting your audience to sleep? Are you looking for something new, real, and exciting for your next corporate event?

If yes—then Robert Channing's Amazing E.S.P. Show is exactly what you need to satisfy the discriminating taste of your audience. Robert's exciting, entertaining, and mind-boggling show will have your audience on the edge of their seats, squirming with anticipation.

How is Robert Channing your solution? Why is he the perfect fit for your needs?

Simply put—**Robert Channing's E.S.P. show is amazing, riveting and clean—with a perfect blend of comedy.** This dramatic yet upbeat program masterfully illustrates the strange and incredible mysteries of the mind. **Your audience will thank you for having Robert's show and you will look great in the eyes of your clients and peers.**

Full audience participation...

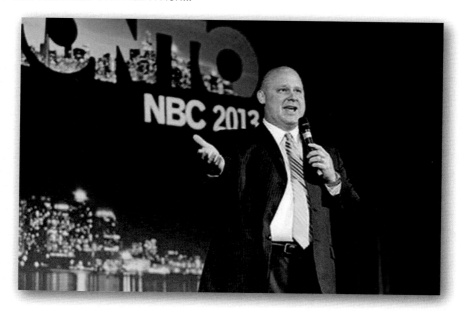

Your whole audience will participate and experience the fascinating and mysterious wonders of the sixth sense. Pick a thought—any thought. Robert will tell you what it is. Social security numbers, special dates, or even the exact amount of money in someone's pocket—it's no challenge to Robert Channing. Your mind will ache with curiosity and wonder. Special thoughts, specific people, special events—if it is on your mind, Robert can reveal these innermost thoughts. He will deliver **all this and more—while maintaining a level of professionalism and sensitivity to the privacy of your audience. Your audience will be entertained and motivated.**

ABSOLUTELY NO AUDIENCE CONFEDERATES...
SATISFACTION GUARANTEED.

No information is ever given to Robert before the performance. The names, numbers, and innermost thoughts that he reveals are those actually held in the minds of the audience—all strangers to him. **Robert offers a 100% full refund** of his fee to anyone who can prove that there are stooges or informants planted in the audience. **We are so confident that you will be nothing less than thrilled with this show—that Robert offers you a money back guarantee.**

Robert will dazzle your audience with his quick wit, amazing mind reading, and fun personality, which will also help you create a fun and exciting atmosphere for your event. He regularly performs at **corporate events, charity events, tradeshows, colleges**, and private events all around the world.

ROBERT CHANNING'S AMAZING ESP SHOW IS SURE TO LEAVE YOUR AUDIENCE AMAZED AND THOROUGHLY ENTERTAINED.

"He knows what you are wearing RIGHT NOW. Don't believe it? Call and see for yourself!"

Call Now (800) 320-9650 or Email Us NOW!!! info@powerperformers.com

Made in the USA
Middletown, DE
15 May 2018